The Mafia in HAVANA

The Mafia in HAVANA

A Caribbean Mob Story

Enrique Cirules

Ocean Press
Melbourne ▪ New York
www.oceanbooks.com.au

Copyright © 2010 Ocean Press
Copyright © 2010 Enrique Cirules

Translated by Douglas E. LaPrade

ISBN 978-0-9804292-3-7
Library of Congress Catalog Card Number: 2010920396

First edition 2004
Revised edition 2010

Originally published in Spanish as *El imperio de la Habana* (Havana: Editorial Letras Cubanas).

Printed in Mexico by Worldcolor Querétaro, S.A. de C.V.

Published by Ocean Press

Australia:　PO Box 1015, North Melbourne,
　　　　　　　Victoria 3051, Australia

USA:　　　511 Avenue of the Americas, #96
　　　　　　　New York, NY 10011-8436, USA
　　　　　　　E-mail: info@oceanbooks.com.au

Ocean Press Trade Distributors:

United States and Canada: **Consortium Book Sales and Distribution**
　　Tel: 1-800-283-3572　　www.cbsd.com

Australia and New Zealand: **Palgrave Macmillan**
　　E-mail: customer.service@macmillan.com.au

UK and Europe: **Turnaround Publisher Services**
　　E-mail: orders@turnaround-uk.com

Mexico and Latin America: **Ocean Sur**
　　E-mail: info@oceansur.com

ocean

www.oceanbooks.com.au
info@oceanbooks.com.au

CONTENTS

Translator's Note

To write this book, Enrique Cirules undertook research in the Archivo Nacional de Cuba, where he examined the records of the Banco Nacional de Cuba. These records and other sources illustrate Cirules's thesis that Cuba's pre-revolution government was manipulated by three U.S. institutions: the Mafia, the intelligence community and the financial sector. Many banks and companies in Cuba served as fronts for Mafia activities, and Cirules offers evidence of such corruption.

A particular document that Cirules found in his research is a letter sent from Allen Dulles, director of the CIA, to Cuba's President Fulgencio Batista on July 15, 1955. In this letter, Dulles thanks Batista for hosting him during a trip to Havana. Then Dulles explains to Batista how Cuban personnel will travel to Washington to discuss anticommunist tactics with the CIA. Cirules located this letter in the archives of Cuba's Ministry of the Interior, and the reader can examine the text of this letter in the following pages.

Cirules's assessment of pre-revolution Cuba is well balanced. Besides his Cuban archival sources, Cirules cites the memoir of Dwight D. Eisenhower, president of the United States at the time of the Cuban Revolution. Cirules also refers to the memoir of Estes Kefauver, who was head of a U.S. Senate committee that investigated the Mafia in 1950-51. Cirules also quotes from the memoir of Earl E. T. Smith, the U.S. ambassador to Cuba at the time of the revolutionary victory.

Cirules's masterful blend of Cuban and U.S. sources is informative and convincing. Apart from its investigative rigor, this book offers the reader a glimpse of life in pre-revolution Cuba. Cirules interviewed people who offer accounts of infamous *mafiosi* such as Meyer Lansky and "Lucky" Luciano. The reader learns what it would have been like to accompany Lansky or Luciano on a night out in Havana.

Douglas Edward LaPrade

Acknowledgments

I want to express my gratitude to Frank Agüero Gómez, ex-director of the newspaper *Bastión*. He encouraged me to write this book, after publishing a series of articles I had written, in collaboration with María Mercedes Sánchez Dotres, about international drug trafficking.

Having accumulated a collection of important oral testimonies about the presence of the U.S. Mafia in Cuba, the most difficult task (for the verification of these sources) was to undertake research based on documents of the era. I was able to accomplish this thanks to the administration of the Archivo Nacional de Cuba and to its specialists and employees. That institution placed in my hands valuable documents from its holdings, and Mayra Mena became an efficient collaborator.

I am indebted to the administration of the Biblioteca Nacional José Martí. I also extend my gratitude to Dr. Lucía Sardiñas, for her invaluable support in the development of this research.

I am grateful to Blas, custodian of the defunct Archivo de Seguridad Social, who also made his knowledge available to me. I am likewise grateful to María Mercedes Sánchez Dotres, who was my close collaborator, not only during the research process, but also in the final stages of the project.

As a matter of sincere thanks and justice, I must say that my study of the U.S. Mafia in Cuba has a great precursor: the book, *El primero de enero y el Hotel Deauville,* written in the 1960s by the former food worker Benigno Iglesias Trabadelo. Born in the northeast of Asturias, Spain, in 1911, Iglesias Trabadelo arrived in the port of Havana in 1927, to initiate a long pilgrimage as tavern employee, bartender and touring chauffeur. In 1947, he began working in the restaurant and cabaret industry in Havana. In 1950, he worked in a bar in Caracas, Venezuela, but returned to Cuba to work in the Cinódromo (dog track) at Marianao Beach, becoming one of the first food workers in the hotels Habana Hilton, Flamingo and Deauville. Although he had direct knowledge of stories relating to important U.S. *mafiosi* in Havana, Benigno's book remains unpublished. I visited him in 1990 and, besides showing me his prized testimonies, Benigno wanted to help with my research, generously offering his book to me.

I am also grateful to the journalist Enrique de la Osa, who left a mountain of extraordinary testimonies about the social, moral and political problems of the Cuban nation. These appeared in articles and chronicles published in the "In Cuba" section of the magazine *Bohemia*. My gratitude to the writer Imeldo Álvarez, who told fascinating stories about the dazzling Havana of the 1950s, introducing me to Amadeo Barletta Barletta, Amleto Battisti y Lora, George Raft and other famous personalities of the Mafia, and of politics of the time.

Dr. Helio Dutra introduced me to the artistic and social world of the era, and my friend Oscar Fernández Padilla offered testimony about the forces that opposed the Mafia groups in Havana.

The following people also offered their testimonies or were consulted at various stages: Luis Cesto, a journalist who provided interesting observations about events leading to the coup d'état of March 10, 1952. Miguel Ángel Domínguez, a member of the commando unit that executed Colonel Blanco Rico in the Montmartre cabaret. (The colonel was chief of the regime's Military Intelligence Services in 1956.) Carlos Dotres García, retired telegraph operator. Aristides Guerra (the "King of Food,") veteran of the Rebel Army. Jorge Ibarra, historian, for his assistance and advice. Julio Le Riverend, the eminent Cuban historian. Neftalí Pernas, a leader in the clandestine operations of the Popular Socialist Party. Juan Portilla, secretary of the sugar industry leader Jesús Menéndez, who was assassinated during the McCarthy-like repression in Cuba, in 1948. Gervasio Reimont, who reached the rank of captain in the secret service of the pseudo republic. In reality, Gervasio Reimont was a revolutionary who had infiltrated the political-military leadership during the 1934-58 period. René Santiesteban Ochoa, retired lawyer. José Sosa ("Pepe"), functionary in the Cuban Ministry of Culture, oral historian of the era. Graciela Tabío, editor at Editorial José Martí. Evelio Tellería, journalist specializing in the Cuban labor movement. Alfredo Viñas, ex-director of Radio Habana Cuba, for his deep knowledge of the world of politics and the so-called high society of Havana. The author also heard the testimonies of many food workers, who had previously served as sources for Iglesias Trabadelo. I would like to thank: Lorenzo Sosa Martínez, Humberto Fernández, Rafael Carballido, Bruno Rodríguez, Juan Rivera, Emilio Martínez Hernández, the grocery-store keeper Prieto, and other employees of hotels, casinos and cabarets in Havana. Portela also brought important references to our notice, not just relying on his own personal knowledge, but by relaying stories preserved through oral tradition.

I wish to thank the dealers, salon employees, canteen operators, elevator operators, parking lot attendants and former chauffeurs or employees who had access to the gambling rooms, salons, private rooms and offices of various individuals. I would also like to thank former bank employees and those people who prefer to remain anonymous witnesses.

Finally, I would like to thank Celina Ríos and her husband Jorge, who generously received me under their roof in the final (and most difficult) months, during which *El imperio de la Habana* (title of the Spanish version of *The Mafia in Havana*) was completed.

The rest remains in my memory.

Introduction

During the years that I worked at the port of Havana, I knew an old ship named *Liberty*, of the Pacific Line, that made repeated trips to the Far East.

The ship had an Indian steward. He was silent, wore a white turban, and had an enormous beard. As soon as the vessel finished docking, he left the trading ship to delve into that labyrinth of bars, canteens, taverns and brothels that proliferated in the area.

In a seaport, unusual revelations can come to light; and that legendary bearded character was an intimate acquaintance of two brothers who managed the most important agency of the port. They were responsible for managing the traffic of the García Line, which sailed to destinations in the Gulf of Mexico. The brothers were very famous and inclined to extravagance, such as driving the latest model Buick and consorting with the beautiful women of the region.

One young employee at one of the canteens of the port earned 25 pesos per month, plus either lunch or supper. The brothers paid for his overnight trips to Havana, a ticket on the express train and return trip the following day. The employee was also paid a tip of 30 pesos, on the condition that he carry some gifts with him. That employee made three, maybe four, trips. The brothers appeared at 7 p.m. at the train station, with two big baskets loaded with fresh fish on ice, plus the fare and his 30 pesos; and bade farewell to their emissary. His assignment was to arrive in Havana, take a taxi to an address on Zanja Street, and deliver the baskets to a person who, without even saying a word, would give the messenger five more pesos as a tip.

The young man, six years older than I, went back out into the street, had breakfast in a small cafe, lodged in a cheap inn, slept three or four hours, woke up at noon, showered, then put on his old second-hand *guayabera* shirt. After eating something, he walked to one of the brothels on Zanja Street to indulge himself, for two pesos. Then, half an hour before the express left for Puerto Tarafa, he arrived at Central Station.

It happened that, on the third or fourth trip, he examined the contents of one basket. He had never done this before, because of the disagreeable odor of the fish. This time, before completing the errand, he searched in the basket until he found the reason for the delivery. He discovered, beneath the fish, several packages wrapped in thick paper, sealed in wax, the kind of packages used to wrap marijuana. Inside were some bars that could have weighed one kilogram each. They were the color of ocher, and had a peculiar, unfamiliar odor.

He had suspected something, after hearing talk. Immediately, after finding the bars, he was certain that he had been made the messenger of pipe dreams, all for three 10-peso bills and his fare on the night express. He returned to the port but did not find either of the brothers. He went to their boss, the sponsor of the trips, Mr. Rasca. But the latter excused himself with a single sentence: none of that was important. In any case, my friend felt betrayed. As he was of a violent disposition, he cornered the boss against a wall and placed a dagger against his neck, while Rasca apologized profusely.

The next day, the local police arrested my friend. They locked him in a cell for a few days, until an officer advised him that the best thing he could do was to work things out with the boss, because the next incident would have serious consequences. He went to see Rasca, who gave him a check for 300 pesos, advised him not to raise the subject with the brothers and to forget the address on Zanja Street. He further advised my friend to buy a used car with the money and become a hired chauffeur, because the boss did not want to see him at his place of business again.

Fifteen years later, I read *The Godfather*, a book that made a strong impression on me. It was not the language, or the structure of the book, or even the plot, but rather a certain wisdom that characterizes its best pages. The way it portrays human enigmas reminded me of certain master painters of the Italian Renaissance.

Puzo's book is set in the United States, beginning in the 1920s, and unfolds historically until it reaches our times. The book was somewhat frustrating, however, for the simple reason that I was already convinced that the Mafia known to Cubans was not the same Mob that Puzo portrays with his singular mastery.

In the case of Cuba, I had learned different stories through friends who knew the dazzling Havana of those days, when Meyer Lansky established the Hotel Riviera. It was extraordinary just how many authors had achieved notoriety and celebrity by writing stories that convinced the public they had penetrated a great mystery. Some of these authors made bold allusions to the fierce presence of a Mafia in Havana, only making the historical study of this problem more urgent.

Yet until now, no systematic study of the Mafia had been made in relation to Cuba. The terrible reality of the U.S. Mafia's presence on the island has just always been accepted.

I had a great deal of information regarding the Mafia in Colombia, and I knew certain people who told convincing stories. In the summer of 1988, I made my first trip to Colombia. It was only a four-week trip, to a country of great contrasts: one that had known the full range of human experiences — violence, love, wealth, misery, beauty, anxiety, anger and tenderness. A year later (in the summer of 1989) I returned to that country that Cubans have always loved so much, this time in the company of my close collaborator María Mercedes Sánchez Dotres. This time, the stay would be much longer, not only in Santa Fe de Bogotá, but also along the coastal region itself. Our second stay (of almost three months) allowed us to get to know a group of intellectuals and to study certain matters vital to a better understanding of the country.

One fond memory is of the wisdom of Professor Rafael Ortegón Paz, the founder of important educational institutions. Professor Ortegón was profoundly concerned with the problems of Colombian students, and he was the author of a lucid study, *Voragine alucinante en la historia de las drogas*. We had excellent talks with Professor Ortegón, who discussed the problem of the international drug trade; and although that was not the objective of our trip, it was interesting to discover the opinions of learned Colombians on the subject.

It was a relevant subject, however, when in June and July of 1989, there began a ferocious international campaign against the Cuban Revolution; this was despite the fact that the traffic and consumption of drugs in our country had been stemmed since the first weeks of

1959. Such attempts to implicate Cuba in that dirty business were handled, as always, in an exemplary fashion by the Cuban nation.

It was then (first in Barranquilla and later in Santa Fe de Bogotá) that I came to understand that one could not write a book about drug trafficking without involving the world of finance, and its ties to the U.S. intelligence services. One must also take into account the Mafia leadership in the United States that, over the years, had become interwoven with the same financial and intelligence forces devoted to attacking and persecuting the Cuban Revolution.

Nevertheless, after publishing a series of articles related to the drug trade, I faced a dilemma. I had sufficient information to write about the problem; but the project would be based on a mass of previously published information: books, magazines, articles and news items that appear each year about drugs and U.S. interests.

I decided to change the entire course of the project. International drug trafficking was not really a Cuban problem, since it had been stamped out in 1959 when the Rebel Army defeated the imperialist power structure imposed on Cuba, thereby bringing social justice and the country's transformation. Little by little, my new focus became clearer. The most important issue was to study how the U.S. Mafia had operated in Cuba, a topic that had not been previously touched upon, at least in any depth. Had the U.S. Mafia's activities in Cuba reached the levels of excess alleged by some authors and filmmakers? Had the Mafia wielded as much power as Cuban word of mouth affirmed? Or was it all just fiction?

I had decided upon the course that my investigation should take. At the start, I only intended to study the famous Mafia characters who chose Cuba as their base, or their eventual residence, and who had left in their wake so many mysteries, myths and unanswered questions.

From the beginning, my investigations revealed that a Cuban bibliography on the subject is almost nonexistent. The activities of the U.S. Mafia had been accorded an incredible discretion, and protected by official shrouding. In most cases, the *mafiosi* had operated with documentation that identified them as men of great prestige in the world of business — controlling banks, running newspapers, operating radio or television stations, or leading important companies or corporations, all outside their purely criminal activities.

Study of the period 1934-58 was aided by a group of witnesses who had known *mafiosi*. Their recollections allowed us to reconstruct the places the mobsters frequented, their meeting places, personal characteristics, behavior, tastes and preferences. Former assistants and bodyguards, friends and women companions also supplied information. But the amazing thing was verifying the level of impunity the criminals had enjoyed, for such a long time, and under the administration of several presidents.

Stories about the Mafia's operations in Cuba seemed so fantastic that, for us, they validated the declaration made by U.S. Senator Estes Kefauver in May 1950, when he began to study the Mafia's activities within the United States. Kefauver characterized the Mafia's activities as "so tremendous and so outrageous a conspiracy that a lot of people simply aren't going to believe it."[1]

Fortunately for us, this was not the decade of the 1950s, and we were in no danger of being misled by the evasions by which the Mafia's dealings were diluted within the United States. I began immediately the exhausting work of verifying each one of the testimonies I had received. This task required use or consultation of the following sources: 1) Vast archival documentation. 2) The existing bibliography on the subject relating to Cuba. Here, in the majority of cases, the references were to foreign authors. We also had to use important economic, political and social texts by Cuban authors, without which it would be impossible to understand the mechanisms of domination over the Cuban nation. Although, it must be noted, the Mafia had been considered until our times a marginal group, as a result of which they were excluded from historical analyses. 3) The press of the period.

The purpose of the study was not just to understand the U.S. Mafia's relationships to, or ties with, the political and military leadership of Cuba. It was also necessary to reflect upon the complex web of interdependent and complementary businesses that the Mafia factions shared, and the interests they had in common with the dominant financial groups in Cuba.

This inevitably led to other questions: How was it possible that a vast criminal organization could operate in Cuba for more than 25 years without inviting the slightest official reproach? What political or financial groups (both within and outside the island) were directly involved in the formation of that criminal state?

It was impossible to comprehend even half the extent of the U.S. Mafia's presence without an in-depth study of the economic, political and social reality of the period. Furthermore, to answer any other significant questions, it was necessary to know which factors (internal and external) made it possible for organized crime from the United States to create a powerful criminal empire in the greatest of the Antilles.

We can now assure readers that the U.S. Mafia's activities in Cuba were not limited to hotels, casinos, drugs or organized prostitution. The most recent studies reveal a more far-reaching project, aimed at successively occupying positions that afforded them ever greater profits. We have made a study of four powerful Mafia families which, beginning in the 1930s, possessed a fabulous network of interests and had many differences with the rest of the U.S. Mafia. These Mafia families were under the charge of Amleto Battisti y Lora, Amadeo Barletta Barletta, the two Santo Trafficantes (father and son), and the most famous of all the *mafiosi* who operated in Cuba: "the Mafia's financier," Meyer Lansky.

In the acknowledgments to this book I include a list of witnesses and consultants, without whom it would not have been possible to successfully complete the research. Oral tradition, as a historical source, was of primary importance.

The witnesses can be classified into three large groups: business-men and intellectuals; revolutionary militants; and employees of the institutions in which the U.S. Mafia operated — including card dealers, chauffeurs and servants. Some employees of hotels and casinos have requested anonymity. Finally, the judgments and opinions of journalists and historians who were consulted have been of great service.

Enrique Cirules

Rumba Heaven!

In 1957, the U.S.-based gangster, Umberto Anastasio (also known as Albert Anastasia), was seen at the terminal of the international airport of Rancho Boyeros — and then in the most diverse places in Havana. He had a leather suitcase, broad-brimmed hat, three-inch belt and open gray suit, and that fierce demeanor that so intimidated people.

Umberto's visit was an intense one. He stayed five or six days in 1957, tossing chips in luxurious casinos, attending the horse races, drinking in one of the familiar bars, always leaving before midnight with the same friends to frequent the most scintillating cabaret on earth.

With its crystal arches, the Tropicana was certainly the most captivating of refuges. It offered the fashionable game of bingo with 10,000 pesos prize-money, a restaurant with exquisite dishes, mulattas and a powerful gaming bank.

Anastasio insisted on seeing everything, to weigh every idea and calculate every risk. He wanted to test the resistance his projects might encounter. The Tropicana's manager Martin Fox welcomed him with absolute attention, so that Anastasio, the director of Crime, Inc., felt completely at home. Fox reserved the best table for him, with an efficient and refined waiter, and there were other pleasant surprises to follow.

During those days, the showmaster Roderico Neyra (Rodney) was celebrating his sixth anniversary — six years of organizing fabulous spectacles. Now the cabaret was staging portions of "Drums over Havana" and scenes from "Tropicana Souvenir."

In New York, they were making arrangements for the ballet company, Pearls of the Orient, to land at the Boyeros airport, with its 25 charming Philippine women and three great stars: Loma Duque, Vivian Thom and Erlinda Cortés. If that were not enough, the return of Nat King Cole was announced. He would receive five grand for every group of three songs performed.

With his face covered in distinctive leopard spots of light, Rodney unleashed a whirlwind of drums and trumpets on the Tropicana stage. Dancers crossed over fake bridges, descended magic stairways and glided over the many ramps, surrounded by smoke, fragrances, crackling noises and flashing lights, creating an interplay of lights and shadows, in a miasma of palms and flowers under the splendor of the stars.

In 1957, the cabaret hosts staged all kinds of fantasies to entice the thousands of U.S. tourists. The latter came to drink and dance, to test their nerve in the casinos, use cocaine, indulge themselves sexually, or satisfy any other desire or preference, however unusual. With the arrival of the moneyed crowd, the taxi drivers and profiteers began to line up; and a legion of assistants, prostitutes in fine clothing and high-class beggars emerged.

The island was the paradise of the rumba dancer, the maraca and rum. Havana was a kingdom of tolerance: anything could be arranged with the greatest of impunity, whether during the bright, hot summers or during the winter months, when ferocious northern gales and sea winds dashed against the coast. In the hotels and dens of luxury, however, the climate was always pleasantly comfortable. On the dance floors, stellar figures paraded, and nights seemed nothing short of endless, always enlivened by scandals, marvels and beautiful songs.

Mario García, manager and publicity agent of the Montmartre casino-cabaret, just a couple of steps from La Rampa Street, had rapidly become an important figure. His infamous cabaret was now closed, however, because of the execution there of Colonel Blanco Rico, Batista's chief of military intelligence services. Rico was surprised and shot upon leaving the elevator. That was slightly more than could be tolerated, and the leading *mafiosi*, housed in the Hotel Nacional, decided to let things cool off a little to avoid making a bad impression on the tourists.

The versatile showman García was dispatched to Caracas with a treat known as "The Thousand and One Nights." The spectacle was staged by the eminent Pedrito del Valle, and there were performances in one of the most exclusive casinos of Venezuela.

The most unforeseeable of scandals would feature the showgirl Zizi de París. Just after her entrance, she suffered a seizure resulting from severe cocaine abuse. It was a truly wild show and cost González Jerez his managerial position at Havana's Sans Souci cabaret, in spite of his not allowing Zizi to return on to the stage.

Rolando Laserie, a successful singer on the circuit, had been brought by his sponsors to a venue run by Santo Trafficante Jr. and was immediately promoted. Though he had a repertoire of only four songs, Laserie was given an orchestra, a publicity campaign and diverse amenities, and was immediately converted into one of the most sought-after singers of the period.

During the horse racing season, the largest bets were made in the Havana racing track. Nights were open to any possibility, depending on whether you won or lost. The biggest spenders usually called for drinks, before dining in some elegant place. From the racing track, or from one of the rooms at the Jockey Club, they ordered their cars and headed for 51st Avenue and the low reddish roof of the Sans Souci.

The Hotel Sevilla Biltmore was also an elegant place, near the very doors of the presidential palace. The Biltmore had bold architecture, and from its large windows and balconies (and through the dense foliage of the trees in the park) one could distinguish parts of the president's palatial mansion. The most powerful person at the Biltmore was the Corsican Amleto Battisti, a Mafia kingpin, in charge of highly intricate affairs. (He was already a member of the House of Representatives.) Amleto took pride in the fact that each month a new shipment of prostitutes came to his hotel for the exclusive enjoyment of his guests.

Havana's future seemed very promising for big business. The inauguration of the luxurious Capri Hotel, on the corner of N Street and 21st Avenue, was scheduled for November 15. With its precious red salon, it housed an extraordinary casino — decorated with lamps, curtains, silks and marbles — overseen by Hollywood actor George Raft. Carlyle, another famous Havana choreographer, was in charge of preparing the Capri's inaugural show.

The fascinating Naja Kajamura arrived to perform the suggestive dances of Brazil and immediately signed a lavish contract to appear twice nightly. The Brazilian combined mystery with fear, allowing, in the middle of her act, several snakes to coil about her body. Other stars enjoyed exceptional fame. Vocalist Lucy Fábregas became a great sensation. She liked the maritime profile of the city, and sang her songs in the Tally Ho. She had no desire to return to Puerto Rico. She had found in Havana a favorable setting for her voice, suitable for her style.

A leading "entepreneur" was Gaspar Pumarejo, flashy maestro of the big swindle. Little was known back then of secret deals Pumarejo was making with crime king Amadeo Barletta. Pumarejo introduced into Cuba an immeasurable passion for strokes of luck. Through television game shows and other forms of gambling, he created a veritable philosophy out of false hopes. Pumarejo sold fantasies of instant wealth, using novel techniques of persuasion.

It was a midsummer night's dream, like flying on a magic carpet. As for the quiz questions, one simply took or left prizes at whim. There was no hint that great cunning was involved. Unforeseen things happened, like great bolts of lightning, that made it all seem spontaneous and reinforced the credibility of Pumarejo's programs.

What a game! That game of chance! Pumarejo even brought the famous actress Marta Ruth to Havana to display her theatrical charms, and assisted by a certain Otto Sirgo she became a stellar hostess. Pumarejo's most resounding success, however, would be when he signed a contract with Renato Carosone.

Carosone arrived in Havana, in triumphant fashion, from Italy. He was 36 years old, and the musical director, pianist, composer and arranger for a group that would become a big hit with Cubans. Advertisements on television affirmed, to music, that anyone could find money hidden in various products. Rina brand soap advertisements promised hard soap and lots of cash. Promotional fanfare suggested that a shiny Pontiac might be hidden beneath the lid of a can. A chronicler of the time wrote:

> Cuba... had been converted into the country of surprises. Win an apartment just by squeezing a tube of toothpaste! Win in the kitchen, waiting for the rice to cook! The lucky ball could appear in the washtub, when scrubbing your clothes with soap. Miracles abounded. If you went to a boxing match, and they began to raise the arm of the winner, yet suddenly the winner was the one knocked out and stretched flat on the floor, you were not to be surprised; because this island was the country of great surprises.[1]

Everything was manipulated. It was a total scam. Even cultivated people resigned themselves to the big lie. In the midst of poverty and misery on the island, diverse forms of deceit became ever more refined, inspiring an ever more bitter hope. In the *New York Times*, in an article published under the name of journalist R. Hunt Phillips, it was reported:

> Gambling attacks Cuba like a storm. Housewives spend their lives cutting coupons and box tops. Game shows have invaded TV with the force of a tropical hurricane... Even the large establishments have succumbed. Every customer receives a coupon for each peso he spends. A country of chance...[2]

It was five years since General Batista had been made the absolute lord of power, in the March 1952 coup, when he entered Camp Columbia to install a bloody dictatorship in Cuba. Certain businesses got along wonderfully with the regime, especially those protected by the exclusive hotels, casinos, restaurants and cabarets.

By the port of Havana, the nightspots grew increasingly sordid. Brothels rapidly increased in number. There were few parts of the city where you couldn't find a drug vendor, a gaming table, a gunman and hundreds of prostitutes.

Fascinating hotels were being opened at this time. They were constructed rapidly, along with beautiful new thoroughfares. Others were built to house the administration of the criminal state, as well as its financial institutions. It was even possible to travel beneath the harbor, through the sensational Havana tunnel, which linked the urban center with the beaches to the east. These were the boldest investments planned by the U.S. Mafia: they would glitter along the banks of the Jaimanitas River all the way to the white sand beaches at Varadero.

In Havana, all was going to plan. The capital had one million inhabitants, thousands of bars and canteens attended by a legion of women. Prostitutes operated "efficiently," from those charging minimum rates to others who could arrange memorable appointments in exclusive mansions ruled by famous madams. Everything was controlled. Marina, figurehead for a chain of brothels, was a public figure of singular importance.

Meanwhile, half the population was in need. It was normal to find an army of beggars in the streets, orphans, sick people and derelicts.

One could find games of chance on every corner: the lucky ball, the lottery ticket, bingo, dice and cards. Marijuana was everywhere. There was no cocaine on the streets, however, because cocaine was considered a drug for the more refined, and consumed only in elegant places.

When he arrived, the heat was furious in Havana; but to the great Umberto Anastasio, the Cuban capital seemed simply charming. Business appeared very promising. The U.S.-based Mafia interests Anastasio represented would simply have to push a little harder. Then everyone would understand that Havana could not remain the exclusive domain of the Mafia families who had already gained a foothold there.

There was nothing to worry about in Cuba. Prison? The authorities were corrupt and tame. Assassination, or rebellion? It seemed of no importance that Fidel Castro had returned in December 1956, after his imprisonment and exile, to the beat of war drums in Oriente.[3] It was known that Castro had landed and that government forces had surprised and almost annihilated them. It was rumored that a few had managed to regroup and that Fidel Castro, ever the warrior, had sought refuge with 12 men in the mountains of the Sierra Maestra.

Toward the middle of that year, constitutional rights were briefly restored. It wasn't much, but it made a slight opening in the ironclad censorship. In just under a week, rumors became certainty. Like the surges of a cyclone, news of death and torture was not limited to regions of Oriente. In Pinar del Río, the tobacco festival ended in gunfire and flames; the army barracks in San Juan y Martínez was burned. Sabotage, fires and explosions were reported in Cienfuegos, Rodas and Camajuaní. The country's highways seemed to be rivers of nails and spikes. Between Güaimaro and Las Tunas, the dead bodies of three young people lay beneath a small bridge. In the sugar mill towns, refineries and villages, flags waved along with posters proclaiming "July 26" [the name of Fidel Castro's rebel movement]; and two peasants in Guantánamo were tortured, then assassinated and hung from a tree. There was a fire in the canefield of Cárdenas. A large bomb exploded in downtown Camagüey; torches destroyed the fields of Jaronú, Cunagua, Jagüeyal, Steward and Ciego de Ávila. The army and police halted the trains of Morón. Two lay dead on the highway to Palma Soriano; there were ambushes in Varadero, Banes and Puerto Padre. Near Mariel, a young black man lay dead after two shots to the head. A mother reported that the army was torturing her son in the Leoncio Vidal Regiment in Santa Clara, and a policeman was injured by gunfire in a Havana park. Meanwhile, in the north of Oriente, Colonel Fermín Cowley declared he was prepared to eradicate every last communist.

According to dispatches sent from Havana by journalist Francis L. Carthey of United Press International, Batista's army had concentrated its troops against the group that had mounted the armed uprising. The army had formed a kind of steel ring around the area where Fidel Castro's guerrillas were based.

The Cuban press also reported the new situation, including in its pages an interview with Colonel Barreras.[4] Barreras issued his famous declaration from the general barracks of the army, the Estrada

Palma sugar mill: "We are here," he said, "and if the rebels decide to strike us, we will liquidate them." Two weeks later, on July 27, 1957, in an action that seemed mysterious to the Batista dictatorship, the fledgling Rebel Army occupied the installations of the sugar mill. The insurgents remained there for two hours, more than enough time for the old barracks at Estrada Palma to go up in flames. The insurgents retreated, and with the first light of dawn, the townspeople began to relate how, before the attack began, they had heard the wild call of the *guamo* shells like a warcry.[5]

It was an exceptional year for the forces of liberation; but for the U.S. Mafia groups that operated from the Hotel Nacional, events on the other side of the Cuban capital still did not seem to represent a real danger. They were distracted by nocturnal parties, or by visits from screen and recording idols from Beverly Hills, Malibu Beach and Bel Air. Scandals also provided distraction. The redheaded Maureen O'Hara was found stretched out over three seats in a theater. The story about Robert Mitchum was even wilder. After smoking a joint, he took off his clothes in the middle of a party. Out of his mind, he doused his body with a bottle of sauce and proclaimed that he was the finest hamburger in Havana. But the greatest scandal concerned two Hollywood stars. Ava Gardner — the legendary femme fatale — was reportedly found with Lana Turner in an illicit encounter, in a private part of Palm Beach.

The Mafia planned everything. Little by little Hollywood's great stars showed up in splendid Havana.[6] The first was Frank Sinatra (crowned that year as a giant of popular entertainment).

During that astonishing year, the U.S. press assured readers that the U.S. Congress was accumulating evidence to imprison the principal Mafia leaders on home soil. In Cuba, however, the bosses Amleto Battisti y Lora and Amadeo Barletta Barletta remained important public figures. They ran a network of untouchable businesses, in which semilegal control merged with gang-style law. In the manipulation of the sugar trade, a certain Julius Wolf excelled. Even the slippery and astute "Mafia financier" Meyer Lansky was seen as an honorable businessman. Mobster heavyweight Luigi Santo Trafficante Jr. was able to portray himself as a pillar of the business world, because the Mafia's contacts and ties reached everywhere, even to the presidential office.[7]

It was early afternoon when Umberto Anastasio showed up at the Copacabana Hotel. He was there for a shrill, three-hour argument with his partners. Some say he came intending to intimidate his rivals; making threats and gestures designed to inspire fear.

Not long after this meeting in Cuba, a bloody image circulated in newspapers around the world. It showed Umberto Anastasio sprawled out on the floor of a glassed-in barber shop in New York.

It happened a little before 10 a.m. on October 25, when two gangsters, their faces covered with scarves, entered through the main door, crossed the lobby of the Hotel Sheraton Park, headed straight for the barber shop and sat down on either side of chair number four. Very calmly, they pointed their guns at Anastasio and shot him dead. The gunmen were about 30 and 35 years old, fashionably dressed, wearing hats with three-inch bands and dark green sunglasses.

A Mafia war erupted. Various rival gangland groups left scores of dead in the principal cities of the United States. U.S. authorities theorized that the conflict was over the immense factional interests held in the Cuban capital.

It was a truly major struggle. The great Mafia families of the Havana empire were pitted against the powerful Mafia groups based in New York. Nobody was willing to be excluded, or pushed aside, when it came to taking a slice of the fabulous profits from Cuba.

The First *Mafiosi* in Cuba

The Mafia in the United States began its activities in Cuba in the early 1920s, running rum and other alcohol. The creation of a giant criminal empire, however, began toward the end of 1933, when first arrangements were made between the recently promoted Colonel Batista and "the Mafia's financier," Meyer Lansky, on direct orders from the great Charles "Lucky" Luciano.

Operations were organized under the supervision of four Mafia families, directed by Amadeo Barletta Barletta, Santo Trafficante Snr., Meyer Lansky and the Corsican Amleto Battisti y Lora.

In 1935, Amleto Battisti occupied the premises of the Hotel Sevilla Biltmore, built at a cost of 2.5 million pesos (in U.S. gold).[1] The hotel had a mortgage dating back to 1922 that was financed by the Citibank Farmers Trust Company. After assuming the mortgage, Battisti established his base of operations in that elegant old tourist center, in Havana's most stately quarter, 100 meters from the presidential palace. Two years later, to finance his many deals, he founded a bank, the Banco de Créditos e Inversiones.

People had good reason to say that the Calabrian Amadeo Barletta Barletta was the "administrator of Mussolini's family in the United States."[2] It was confirmed that he was an undercover spy (in reality, a double agent) planted in the Caribbean region. It is certain that the FBI included him on its blacklist of February 7, 1942. They ordered his arrest and confiscation of his property, but he was tipped off by the Mafia-intelligence groups based in Havana and escaped the island to take secret refuge in Argentina.

When World War II ended, Barletta appeared again in the Cuban capital, this time as a representative of big U.S. companies. He became a financial authority within the country. He was a representative for General Motors buses and trucks, and sales agent for Cadillac, Chevrolet, Oldsmobile and other automobile manufacturers. He was also an important stockholder in pharmaceutical laboratories. He constructed the building on Infanta Street and the Malecón known as Ambar Motors. He started Channel 2 on Cuban television and controlled the newspaper *El Mundo*. With the backing of the Banco Atlántico, he very quickly accrued a dizzying array of businesses, with scores of fake companies serving as fronts.[3]

Santo Trafficante Snr.'s presence in Cuba dates back to when Lansky was holding secret discussions with Colonel Batista.[4] Trafficante had much experience as a gambling organizer in the south of the United States, and soon became Lansky's assistant.

In 1940, Lansky himself returned to New York. (He was about to become a player in deals made between the U.S. Mafia and U.S. secret services during World War II.) Trafficante then came to control all of the Mafia's business in Cuba.

During that period, Trafficante also took charge of training undercover agents within various Cuban political groups, in order to administer Mafia affairs in Havana. During the 1930s, business in the Cuban capital was run directly by *mafiosi* with Sicilian, Corsican, Jewish or U.S. origins. Beginning in the 1940s, however, Cuban nationals were incorporated into the management scheme,[5] although they did not become bosses. This arrangement allowed the Mafia to control not only the apparent power on the island, but also the leadership of opposition groups that represented future political options.

Without a doubt, the most important of all the *mafiosi* in Cuba was the second chief of the U.S. Mafia, Meyer Lansky, the creator and head of the "empire of Havana." He was a Jew born in Grozno, in the south of Czarist Russia (at that time, in Polish territory), taken by his parents to the United States in 1911. Originally named Maier Suchowijansky, he abbreviated and Americanized his surname to Lansky.

Lansky is worthy of special attention by historians. It must be clearly understood that, from the 1930s until the end of 1958, no significant political event or big business deal occurred in Cuba without his involvement, either through secret negotiations, the intervention of Lansky's secret agents, or his actions as an adviser.

Lansky was a man of practical intelligence, ingenious and persuasive, who preferred to operate from the shadows. He had been a great friend of Lucky Luciano since childhood. They went to the same school, and as adolescents became involved in criminal organizations in New York.

These gangster groups accumulated great fortunes in the United States during Prohibition. Between 1930 and 1931 (after the death of Joe "the Boss" Masseria y Maranzano), Lucky Luciano took up the task of reorganizing the old Mafia rooted in the United States. This criminal network consisted of more than 100 gangs of diverse origin, divided into the 24 larger groups that make up today's U.S. Mafia.

Deals made between the U.S. Mafia and Colonel Batista at the end of 1933 would be recalled as follows:

> Lansky made his trip to Havana, met with the Cuban strongman… and came away with gambling rights… including control of the already established casino at the Hotel Nacional… Another [venture] was into legitimate enterprises.[6]

To understand how Cuba became a state at the service of the American Mob, the repeated attempts by the United States to take control of the island, by either purchasing it or by annexing it, must be examined.

Repeated attempts throughout the 19th century are neatly summarized in a fragment of a letter sent from Washington, D.C., to the general of the U.S. troops poised in 1897 for a military assault on Cuban soil:

> The Cuban people are indifferent in the matter of religion, and as a result, the majority are immoral; they are given to great passion and are very sensual; and because they have only the vaguest notions of right

and wrong, they are inclined to seek enjoyment not through work but through violence; and a logical result of this lack of morality is a lack of respect for life. Clearly the immediate annexation to our federation of such disturbing elements in such a great number would be madness, and before considering it we should purge the country, albeit by the means that Divine Providence applied to Sodom and Gomorrah. We must destroy whatever our cannons reach with iron and fire; we must enforce the blockade until hunger and pestilence, constant companions, decimate their peaceful population.[7]

The 20th century, therefore, began for Cuba with a set of economic, political and social impositions, from the moment of the first military intervention by the United States. The power of the battered Creole oligarchy was usurped and it became increasingly dependent, allowing U.S. imperialism, in an accelerated manner, to realize the process of domination over the Cuban economy. This was achieved between 1902-33, the years known as the protectorate period,[8] during which time Washington's foreign policy toward Cuba was implemented through repeated military interventions or threats of intervention, authorized by the Platt Amendment. U.S. ambassadors based in Havana and so-called "proconsuls" intervened when the U.S. Government needed resolutions to messy situations. During this period, Cuba was governed almost without exception by front men for U.S. interests. Still, this power scheme, imposed on the Cuban nation during the first third of the century, exhausted itself definitively by the end of the 1920s because of the power struggle the United States encountered in Cuba.

The new historical period, which began with the overthrow of Machado's dictatorship, has been analyzed by its most ominous protagonist, Fulgencio Batista, to justify his actions against the interests of the Cuban people:

> When the sergeants' revolution triumphed in September 1933, under our direction, Cuba was in the process of becoming a soviet-like republic. Disorder; murder with impunity in the streets; hundreds of groups and sectors acting with authority; the lack of character and moral courage of the government, imposed under the protection of the Platt Amendment, to command the army and the police, which themselves were in a state of

disintegration; the anarchy in the labor sector and the collapse of the frail economy that still remained, constituted the atmosphere for a small but well-organized communist group. In some workplaces the soviets had already established themselves, and the burial of Julio Antonio Mella in Havana on September 29 of that year, after he had been assassinated in Mexico years before, was the pretext for duplicating the coup d'état that Trotsky had mounted against Kerensky.

The blossoming army and the democratic spirit that we imposed on the September Revolution fought bravely to expel the Kremlin's disciples from the sugar mills and other workplaces. In the memoirs of Ambassador Sumner Welles there is evidence of our firm attitude against the reds.

After about five years, Cuba was submerged in a period of conspiracies, criminal activities, terrorism and agitation. Then, as later, ambitious individuals and organizations rejected the ballot boxes. The general elections of 1936 did not bring peace. Both the elections and the peace were sabotaged by the communists, by their enthusiastic companions, and by those who just went along through lack of understanding. In this state, the communists and those other political and revolutionary organizations adopted the slogan, "Constitution First," opposing the holding of new elections, and as our purpose was to pursue peace and institutional stability, we took their word for it…

Neither the democratic parties upon which I based my candidacy, nor I as a leader, produced at any time protests that could be identified with that [communist][9] doctrine nor did we share any of its tendencies.[10]

After September 4, 1933, the revolutionary forces were gaining positions by which they might realize a radical turn in the historic development of the Cuban nation. For that reason, the U.S. intelligence bodies accelerated the reordering of the traditional power structures in Cuba.

From 1934 onward, new imperial forces entered Cuba. In just a few years, they managed to build a complex network, directed at neutralizing the aspirations of the Cuban people, as the state rapidly conformed to the worst influences of the American Mob.

Operations were linked to the political and military leaderships of various presidents. Study of this period reveals some general characteristics that apply to this complex and apparently contradictory period of Cuban society.

Firstly, at the start of the 1930s, there was an accelerated penetration of the Cuban economy by financial groups, controlled by the Rockefeller family (in its two branches, headed by John and William). A good example is the Standard Oil Company of New Jersey.[11] The Rockefellers used a banking and commercial complex of great magnitude (Citibank, Chase National Bank, and later the Chase Manhattan Bank) to reinforce imperial domination in essential parts of the Cuban economy. Other groups included the Americanized German Schroeder Bank and the Sullivan & Cromwell financial complex, in which brothers John and Allen Dulles were prominent. All had sinister origins and were characterized by bribery, blackmail and violence perpetrated against competitors.

This phenomenon has still not been studied sufficiently, considering the magnitude of the financial interests in play, which so strongly left their mark on Cuban political and social events of the period.

The second essential characteristic was the entrance of the recently organized U.S. Mafia into Cuba. The U.S. Mafia was not at this stage just a marginal group, in terms of the domination of Cuban society. Nor was the Mafia's power and control of the island the result of the coup d'état of 1952. Rather, that event was merely the Mafia's coronation.

From the beginning, the Cuban capital offered the U.S. Mafia the most splendid of paradises, with its tourism and organized gambling, under the direction of the Mafia families of Amleto Battisti, Amadeo Barletta, the two Santo Trafficantes and Meyer Lansky. These families directed criminal empires in Havana, which accelerated in growth until around 1940, when Cuba had become one of the most important centers of international crime.

Between 1937 and 1940, Lansky settled permanently in Cuba to found "a true empire of nine casinos and six hotels."[12] The restaurant worker Benigno Iglesias Trabadelo tells us, in his unpublished book of memoirs, how:

> The U.S. Mafia, from the first quarter of the 20th century, operated the casinos in the tourist hotels, in the cabarets, in the entertainment centers, in the aristocratic clubs and even in the quarters where there were

neighborhood gambling houses. This is confirmed by Stephan Yluck Klein (Estéfano), who was known as a great gastronomic expert, a true professional who, since the 1930s, taught us so much. Estéfano came to Cuba under contract with the Cuban American Realty Company (a front)[13] which began to operate alongside other enterprises: the Hotel Sevilla Biltmore, the Gran Casino Nacional, the Summer Casino, the Chateau Madrid, the Sans Souci, the Havana race track, La Concha, the Havana Biltmore Country Club and others. The Gran Casino Nacional was the most ostentatious in the Americas. Its Muses went to the Tropicana when the Havana Country Club bought it, to annex its property.[14]

The Mafia began to operate in the race track, where horse races, tourism and betting converged. Popular gaming likewise came under the control of the Mafia. In the same way they controlled banks, the Mafia founded airline companies (allowing the age of cocaine to begin in Cuba). They also set up financial bodies, insurance companies and import and export houses. Many deals took place in an unusual pyramid scheme[15] in the spheres of commerce, industry, transportation, communications — press, radio and television — and, of course, political leadership.

In keeping with the economic power it had achieved, the U.S. Mafia forces were able to destabilize and partly control Cuba. Considering the volume of their operations, it is presumed that the profits garnered by the empire of Havana were much more substantial than those obtained by the rest of the Cuban economy.

The U.S. intelligence services constituted a third force that began to operate directly in Cuban society. If military intervention or threats of intervention had been common before 1933, they increased to the same degree that the domination and corruption of the Cuban state increased (and the rebelliousness of the people grew). U.S. intelligence did not just observe the events. Rather, in close alliance with the dominant financial groups and the Mafia families in Havana, the U.S. intelligence services used treacherous methods to manipulate important events in Cuba.

This new scheme of imperial domination was reinforced significantly after arrangements were made in the United States in 1942 between the U.S. Mafia and the U.S. intelligence services,[16] and had immediate repercussions in Cuban affairs.

The U.S. intelligence services gained further prominence after 1952 as the revolutionary movement, directed by Fidel Castro, gained in strength and prestige. The networks of the Central Intelligence Agency (CIA) and other special agencies of the United States gradually extended their power. Lyman Kirkpatrick, director of the CIA, was granted exceptional powers by the U.S. Government, and made repeated trips to Havana, beginning in 1955, to lend his support to the dictatorship run by General Batista.[17]

The triumvirate of forces — financial groups, the Mafia and U.S. intelligence — constituted the most diabolical presence on the island, and they were directly responsible for a process that would result in the formation of a criminal state.

A study of this phenomenon demonstrates that between 1937 and 1940 there was already in Cuba an extraordinarily "flexible" state, in which all was pardonable, permissible, tolerable. The state became a tool for the interests of U.S. imperialism, and increasingly more repressive of the aspirations of the Cuban people. In a few years, Havana became a haven for the enjoyment of wealthy tourists, and big operations made transactions through banks installed in the Cuban capital, with fortunes that were illegal in the United States flowing through their ledgers.

As early as 1937, the Chase National Bank financed the Mafia's interests in the Havana race track.[18] Money laundering schemes were common, with the participation of the National City Bank of New York.[19] It must be remembered that the banks effected these operations with no control from the Cuban Government. If any such operation was discovered, excuses for lack of professionalism were made, and that was sufficient. Another case was the reordering of the affairs of the Barletta family, effected by The Trust Company of Cuba, when Barletta took over the Banco Atlántico in 1954.[20] Around 1949, a safe box containing $1 million arrived almost daily in Cuba from the United States. It was addressed to the Banco Gelats.[21] Documentary evidence exists proving that the Mafia also operated directly in the Banco Financiero, which was controlled by an individual who ran a veritable sugar empire.[22] These few examples typify the multiple and complex entanglements between the financial groups and the Mafia.

Batista, the Great Elected One (later, the Great Elector), went rapidly from clerk-typist sergeant to colonel, from chief of the army to major general, in a complex and often politically crude process, in which he disposed of several presidents before installing himself in the presidency in 1940.

The explanation for his whirlwind political success can be found in the exceptional circumstances that the Cuban nation was experiencing.

At that time, imperialist forces launched a series of political maneuvers directed at neutralizing or repressing popular rebellion, and Batista was the most suitable person to implement these measures internally. The ex-sergeant demonstrated that he was capable of guaranteeing these objectives. His actions were successful essentially because the new pro-imperialist forces installed in Cuba were experiencing an accelerated rise to power in U.S. society itself.

In the events leading up to World War II, the affairs of these forces came together with a truly frightful cohesion. To stay in power during that entire period, Batista had to legalize the operations of the empire of Havana to the extent that there was an extraordinarily favorable climate for new financial groups. In the internal order, ferocious repression was unleashed. A series of maneuvers was undertaken that resembled the U.S. imperialist approach to international events of the time. A study of the 1930s would include operations and maneuvers leading up to and during World War II, as well as the skirmishes at the Hotel Nacional, the assassination of Antonio Guiteras and the brutal repression of the strike of March 1935.

The years 1937 to 1938 are vital to an understanding of this complex period of Cuban society. The scheme imposed by the United States — the financial groups, the Mafia and U.S. intelligence services — was such that many reacted with confusion and almost fear, as a result of maneuvers initiated by Batista as the "visible head" of the apparent power.

As Eduardo R. Chibás wrote in 1937, in regard to Batista's scheme to implement the Law of Sugar Coordination and Mortgage Moratorium:

These propositions without a doubt have strong revolutionary implications. Not so long ago, someone else who supported those laws was accused of being a communist and sent to jail. Now Batista has made those laws his. The project is directed at powerful interests that, within the colonial model, have an economic hegemony they would not surrender without a battle, and without defending themselves with all the arms within their reach. In reality, for the time being, those interests do not feel restless; they do not believe in the sincerity of the revolution. They see in the Triennial Plan a process by which Batista justifies his maintenance of power and the suppression of political activities. They cannot conceive that Batista might renounce his alliance with them, or renounce the comfortable and placid workings of the established order for the more responsible role of social reformer.[23]

In Cuba, Batista worked the strings of imperialist power in triumphant fashion, advised by the U.S. intelligence services. When the U.S. president, Franklin D. Roosevelt, returned from a meeting in Teheran, he brought a document regarding a matter he considered extremely important. During the war, Marxist ideas had been widely disseminated in the Antilles; in spite of the antifascist alliances, U.S. intelligence considered its most important objective in Cuba at the time to be the repression of communists and the labor movement.

The most frightening aspect of all this was the way the U.S. Government reacted. Roosevelt would not hand this delicate mission over to the agencies of the United States, or even to his ambassador in Havana, Spruill Braden. Rather, he entrusted the matter to the "financier" Meyer Lansky, because the Mafia's relationship with Batista was so close that:

...when President Franklin D. Roosevelt wanted to convince the Cuban dictator not to run in the 1944 election, Lansky was chosen as the U.S. intermediary. Batista's methods as dictator were already well known and the United States couldn't risk a rebellion on the island at that point in the war. Lansky accomplished his mission and Grau San Martín was elected president of Cuba.[24]

A full study of how these arrangements were implemented between Batista's supporters and those of the Auténtico Party — advised by the Mafia and the U.S. intelligence services — has yet to be carried out. Certainly, in order to take power, Grau had to agree to several compromises, such as including in his government a vice-president who did not have a past association with the Auténtico Party.

Dr. Grau San Martín came to office at an extremely complex and terribly dangerous time. The forces with which he compromised would smooth his road to power. The U.S. Government, its intelligence services, and the U.S. Mafia, in addition to a group of select troops that protected Batista's interests, would impose the conditions.

An analysis of the events reflects that Grau had certain doubts about the maneuvers that his new friends could effect. Would they really let him occupy the presidency? Would they allow him to stay long in the presidential palace? Grau, a professor of physiology, did not have a reputation as a tough politician. For that reason, some did not understand what was really happening with those "inexplicable" alliances.

Batista, however, surprised everybody. He followed the project of the "invisible heads" to the letter of the law. The U.S. press itself did not think he was capable of assuming a role on the fringes of power, and expressed its admiration at his extraordinary flexibility.

The first six months of 1944 (on the road leading to the elections) were marked by some great surprises. Batista emerged with a new image as a great democrat, even in the international press. In his past were 11 years of felonies and abject intrigues. Now Batista amazed everyone with his exaggerated courtesy and proper behavior, which he displayed during the electoral campaign.

Contrary to logic, the general became an advocate of Dr. Ramón Grau San Martín. The first thing Batista did was to order his politicians and military leaders not to attack Grau under any circumstance. It was his wish to carry out the most democratic elections that had ever been held in the history of the republic; he subtly ensured Grau suffered no misfortune.

During those days, secret and extraordinary maneuvers were effected, in which efficient aides-de-camp took part. Eugenio

Menéndez, one of the president's favorites, accompanied him to important meetings, both secret and public. Other contacts fell to Jaime Marimé, Batista's private secretary; and arrangements with the press were managed by Antonio D'Torra, a cheerful sort, who was the very picture of good-natured affability in his broad brimmed hat. It was said that, after coming into the favor of those in power, he had forgotten his old friends.

One of the more perceptive journalists noted at the time that something strange was happening in Cuban politics:

Inexplicably, General Batista always ensures that his friends maintain genteel relations with Dr. Ramón Grau San Martín.

One day in 1940, the Socialist Democratic Coalition candidate got into his black car, listened to the conga *"Batista presidente"* on the radio and drove to 17th Avenue and J Street to pick up Dr. Grau. They drove to the palace, where there was an interview arranged with the chief of state, Dr. Laredo Brú. (Of course, when Grau entered the president's car, the chauffeur turned off the radio.) Both candidates entered the palace through the door on Refugio Street and, smiling, ignored the questions of journalists who waited for the two politicians. Grau was wearing a white "crash" suit, Batista wore raw denim and a Panama hat, and the two moved among the reporters and others who showed up just to be seen by the candidates. Batista did not waste the opportunity to praise Dr. Grau. In response, Grau spoke briefly, offering some veiled tributes to Fulgencio Batista. The gallantry had intimidated the leader of the Auténtico Party so much that he promised, later unfulfilled, that "if General Batista were elected, I would be the first to congratulate him." Batista said the same regarding the head of the PRC. When the interview was finished, the two leaders walked up a marble staircase to be received on the second floor by Dr. Laredo, who conducted them to the Hall of Mirrors. Their portrait was taken, and one of the photographs, in which General Batista appears clasping the left hand of Dr. Grau, with Colonel Laredo in the background, was distributed widely throughout the republic when, days later, the candidate of the CSD traveled around the nation on a political campaign.

Once he occupied the presidency of the republic, General Batista — in spite of his caustic speeches against Grau during his presidential interlude — suggested to his friends that they should try to be courteous to him. We are aware of recent instances in which the president used his influence to prevent attacks on his main political adversary. What is behind all this?[25]

For the political transition of 1944, all measures were employed, from those that had the sheen of absolute legality, to outright tricks. Study of these events leads us to the conclusion that, from January 1944 to November 1958, the U.S. policy toward Cuba was characterized by collaboration between the U.S. intelligence services and the U.S. Mafia families in Havana. It was during Roosevelt's term that this began, with the unrestricted support of General Batista. In 1944, however, when the time came to designate the person who would serve as the guarantor of the new political arrangements in Havana, Roosevelt's action was decisive in sealing the fate of Cuba.

As a consequence, Batista ordered that the elections be strictly democratic. After 11 years of power, he declared from the palace, in a speech delivered before 25,000 people, that the Cuban people had waited a long time for true democracy, and would finally see that day of liberty.

Orders were delivered to the colonels in charge of the provincial regiments, to the captains that commanded the municipal squadrons, and to lieutenants, sergeants and officers in charge of the sugar refineries and sugar producing towns and settlements. Orders were also given to the politicians and bureaucrats, whose responsibility it was to direct and control the elections. Nothing and nobody could interfere with or manipulate the election results in any way.

It was something that had never occurred on the island. In an article in the Cuban press, the following observation of Batista's democratic spirit was made:

> …President Batista has taken care to make known his patriotic objective to all the bureaucrats and armed forces. Without his precautions… political passions perhaps could have misdirected others from the true course, clouding the picture, but his presidential foresight has resulted in something whiter than ermine.[26]

Nevertheless, to avoid appearing suspicious, Carlos Saladrigas was designated as the candidate to oppose Dr. Grau San Martín. Saladrigas was an absolutely incompetent and frustrated politician. He had been prime minister during the early stages of the semi-parliamentarian regime. Because Batista had total confidence in Saladrigas, for a time he presided over the Council of Ministers. He was called upon at various occasions, proving himself an incapable politician, with neither the charisma nor the prestige required to win such an election. If that were not enough, an advertisement showed him photographed between two flags; the Cuban on one side and the U.S. flag on the other. Who in Cuba would vote for someone who presented himself that way? Furthermore, Saladrigas was seen by all as being of the same mold as Batista, whom the people sincerely loathed.

In the last months of 1944, alliances and divisions formed among the parties that favored the Auténtico Party. It goes without saying that unfavorable psychological conditions were encouraged by the scarcities and difficulties brought by World War II, which themselves were accentuated by dirty tricks, a black market and fraudulent business dealings. Responsibility for all this would fall upon the government's candidate.

It was undeniable that the political opposition had been able to establish itself by trading on the prestige that Dr. Ramón Grau San Martín had achieved during his long years of reticence toward the Batista regime. The astonishing thing was that, for those elections, Batista put into practice the direct, secret and obligatory vote. He also assured the neutrality of the army, and gave strict orders for the administration of an electoral process that, in contrast to a long tradition, should now be carried out without pressure, gunshots or a coup d'état.

After the transfer of political power, *Time* magazine published an article that was also reproduced in Cuba. There it was recalled, with more than a little cynicism, that no Cuban government candidate had lost an election since 1933, because those governments had been elected with the consent of the United States.

The U.S. ambassador in Havana, Mr. Braden, put a new formula into effect, which in the future would govern his country's politics with Cuba. Braden expressly forbade, in the name of his government, any U.S. citizen who had businesses or interests on the island to designate funds for the upcoming elections, something that until then had been common practice.

Paradoxically, to justify this measure, people began to talk about "the political maturity of the Cuban democracy."

It was already a tradition for U.S. companies, or U.S. citizens in Cuba — those with investments in the sugar industry, communications, banks, mines, land or any other sector of the Cuban economy — to designate money toward the election of government candidates, with whom the Americans already had long-standing relations.

In the 1944 elections , the U.S. Mafia introduced a new element: an arrangement with all parties. Braden, fulfilling the orders given by Roosevelt, initiated a plan to erase the image of a United States that always intervened in the internal politics of Cuba. It was a great farce. Everybody must have thought that Dr. Ramón Grau San Martín reached the presidency in a climate of extraordinary democracy. In reality, Braden coordinated many other maneuvers, not just involving U.S. citizens but also British subjects living on the island, so that they all abstained from helping Batista's candidate. Due to Braden's actions, Saladrigas stopped receiving the substantial funds that U.S. companies had formerly given to the government candidate's campaigns.

It was calculated that Ambassador Braden prevented almost US$3 million from reaching the hands of the coalition promoting the Saladrigas candidacy. It was an extraordinary sum during the years of World War II and aided the ascent of the Auténtico Party leadership.

The armed forces offered a homage to the president-elect in the Columbia Officers' Club; five days later Grau left for the United States at a personal invitation from Roosevelt. Grau had a stopover in Miami, where he was receptive to the advice and suggestions of the "invisible heads," and the next day continued to Washington. Meanwhile, Batista prepared to abandon the presidential palace. He sent Major Mariano Faget from Cuba to the United States, to undertake studies in the specialized centers of the FBI. Faget had been one of his most faithful and efficient policemen (attached to the U.S. intelligence services); he had stood out for his skillful repression of the enemies of the regime and for his good relations with Meyer Lansky. Faget had conducted beatings and torture, but there was still a long road ahead, so Batista would not leave him behind.

With the sound of marches and a thousand rockets, Grau San Martín assumed power. The bells tolled and the salvos of the mountain artillery thundered from the fortress of La Cabaña, so much so that a crowd eager to witness the official transfer of power to the Auténtico Party invaded the Avenue of Las Misiones.

A month later, during Grau's visit to the United States, the journalist Eladio Secades, with biting humor, affirmed that:

> In Cuba there are two things that a president elect cannot fail to do. Eat with the Rotarians. Make a visit to the United States. The candidate to the presidency who gets the electoral majority receives a place at a banquet in the Hotel Nacional, and a round trip ticket to Washington. We think that the U.S. Government's invitation should always be for the first days of October. That way, the president-elect, as well as visiting the White House and the tomb of the unknown soldier, can also see the games of the World Series.[27]

The joy of the people was immense. They were unaware that old supporters of Machado, supporters of Batista, intelligence agents of the United States and elements with ties to the U.S. Mafia would assume the Auténtico Party leadership. Grau's promises were such that, within a few weeks of his arrival at the palace, he was defended wholeheartedly by only three people who were (and would be) strategically bound to General Batista. They were General Francisco Tabernilla Dolz (from the fortress of La Cabaña) and the senators Santiaguito Rey Pernas and Guillermo Alonso Pujol, Batista's adviser since 1937.

Lucky Luciano and the Cocaine Era

Lucky Luciano used Cuba as a midway point for drug shipments. The island was conveniently located between his heroin suppliers and consumer markets in the United States. Representing these drug channels in Havana was the Corsican Amleto Battisti y Lora.

On occasions, Battisti appeared in the company of the president of the republic of Cuba. He was known and accepted as a prestigious businessman, in industry and finance.[1] As a foreigner (and in spite of his notorious Mafia activities), Battisti even obtained parliamentary immunity through the Liberal Party.

The Mafia found Havana to be its safest stop on the drug route. If drugs made it to the Cuban capital, they were virtually in the United States, by means of heavy air and maritime traffic. Not only were military airports used to ship drugs, but also private runways belonging to high political and military officials of the Batista-Auténtico Party, built on an increasing number of estates in the western provinces.

The U.S. Mafia began the cocaine era in Cuba 30 years before the drug became popular in the United States. At that time, heroin was the most consumed drug in the United States; and the introduction of South American cocaine to U.S. drug markets would have represented an open challenge to Lucky Luciano's heroin interests in the United States by Mafia families in Havana.

It is precisely with the rise to power of the Auténtico Party that the U.S. Mafia in Cuba organized the traffic and consumption of cocaine in Havana. The Auténtico Party came to power when the criminal state was already up and running. This party understood the political compromises it had made. To facilitate drug trafficking, the U.S. Mafia created, among other means, an airline company called Aerovías Q, which was at first the domain of Dr. Indalecio Pertierra, a member of the House of Representatives from the province of Las Villas. Pertierra also ran other operations (in partnership with his two brothers, nicknamed Tuto and Coky), including the Oriental Park race track in Marianao.

From the time of its founding in 1945, Aerovías Q operated from military airports. It used fuel, replacement parts, maintenance staff and pilots of the Cuban Air Force, with the express authorization of President Grau San Martín. From early on, Aerovías Q made a weekly flight: Havana-Camagüey-Barranquilla-Bogotá. A powerful laboratory in Medellín produced "powder" destined for Santo Trafficante Snr.; but everything indicates that this intrigue involved the participation of certain figures of the Auténtico Party in Camagüey, who were associated with pharmaceutical laboratories or drugstores. The Camagüey contacts were an essential link in the drug trade. The cocaine did not always reach the Cuban capital in a direct manner. Rather, the shipment was transferred at the Camagüey airport.

Very soon, it was easy to acquire a small paper wrapper of "powder" in the proliferating network of Havana nightspots. Because of the high consumption of cocaine, earnings proved to be better than could be obtained from the sugar industry. Such was the growth of the drug industry that, at the beginning of the 1940s, international organizations began to make important evaluations of the role of the island in the traffic and consumption of drugs. Based on some of these considerations, Antonio Gil Carballo, in 1944, made the following denunciation:

> The traffic of drugs into our country is growing increasingly alarming, not just in the capital of the republic, but in the furthest corners of the island. The vice of narcotics has found thousands of practitioners, without a doubt the result of official carelessness in repressing this monster, whose

tentacles are devouring the most valuable possession of the population: its youth.

I have been calling attention to the gravity of this problem for more than eight years... This criminal situation grows worse because a few scoundrels occupying high official positions profit in a cowardly way from this immoral situation... I have even made known the guilty involvement of certain authorities... It has all been to no avail and the vice continues to escalate, the powerful traffickers continue rapidly along the way without danger, avoiding judicial problems...

The traffic has been so elevated that Cuba has achieved FIRST PLACE in global statistics...[2]

Havana had become a place where the *mafiosi* made their presence ever more apparent. From 1934-44, the state's activities (especially its relations with the Mafia) had been managed with a certain amount of discretion under Batista, but under the Auténtico Party Government, the Mafia families in Havana began to operate shamelessly. They slowly abandoned the security measures originally imposed by Lansky when the empire of Havana was being created.

At the conclusion of World War II, the U.S. Government lifted Lucky Luciano's sentence, in recognition of his services to U.S. democracy. But Luciano wanted to reestablish himself in New York, to continue managing his deals. Everything indicates that other Mafia interests, headed by Vito Genovese (who aspired to become the U.S. Mafia's new chief), secretly negotiated for Luciano to be deported to Sicily, never to return.

Luciano secretly abandoned Sicily in June 1946, after remaining in his native country for several months. He crossed the Bay of Naples and moved into the luxurious Hotel Excelsior in Naples. After bureaucrats arranged new documents, he moved again, secretly, this time to Rome, occupying a luxurious suite on the Via Veneto.

It was in early autumn when Luciano received a sealed and encoded message. It had been several weeks since he had heard any news from New York, and very little from Havana. The message he received was unclear. It said: "December, Hotel Nacional."

The words were disconcerting. What did Meyer Lansky mean? Perhaps the grand meeting with the entire brotherhood, which

Lansky had arranged, would take place in December? Maybe the arrangements being made in Cuba could only be confirmed in December?

Luciano's conversation with the courier was even more unnerving. The messenger was an old friend, who brought fresh news. It seemed the *capos* who ruled the most important Mafia families in the United States were becoming hopeful because Genovese, in New York, had begun to act as though Luciano was never going to return.

Luciano had two passports, both legal, in the name of Salvatore Lucania. He had a stack of visas, including a new visa allowing him to enter Cuban territory.

The vice-consul of Cuba in Rome sent him the documentation the morning of September 19, 1946, and Luciano left that very afternoon on a flight to Barcelona. Four days later, he caught a plane to Lisbon. The plane in which Luciano crossed the ocean did not fly to Mexico, or to Venezuela, or Colombia, or any of the Caribbean islands, but to one of the most beautiful cities in Brazil.

Later, erroneous, accounts of Lucky Luciano's travels en route to Havana have their origin, no doubt, in the numerous visas he carried. In 1946, the U.S. Mafia did not have significant ties to the main countries of South America — with the exception of some connections known to Lansky and to Santo Trafficante Snr.

It is probable that Luciano planned to make contact with cocaine producers and other business intermediaries.

Luciano arrived at the Rio de Janeiro airport on September 27. It was a prologue to what he would find on the fabulous island of palm trees and rumba, the only difference being that in the Cuba of Ramón Grau San Martín, everything was legal, lasting and stable. It was a world which would afford Luciano the greatest impunity.

A few days later, Lucky was in Havana. He entered Cuba through the international airport of Camagüey, on a direct flight from Brazil. It is debatable whether Meyer Lansky knew the date and place of his arrival. Some, who for obvious reasons prefer to remain anonymous, assure us that Lansky was surprised. Others in the Havana network affirm that it was Luciano himself who was surprised. He had not announced his arrival, but as soon as he left the plane there were several luxury cars waiting for him alongside the runway. Meyer Lansky was also waiting, with several bodyguards.

The two mobsters ate lunch at the Grand Hotel, the most famous in the country's interior. From the dining terrace, they could see the whole city, with its winding streets, bell towers and gray roofs. The lunch was exquisite and accompanied by good Santiago rum. At night they attended a dinner in the country house of the local minister, who owned the big drug store on Avellaneda Street, and ate black beans, rice *a la marinera*, Creole salads, avocado, pineapple and juicy cuts of roast pork.

Besides a Sicilian bodyguard, the local police captain was present, as were several townspeople. When Luciano arrived in Havana, he entered the Hotel Nacional in heavy rain, surrounded by the strong winds and crashing thunder of a tropical storm. Some years later, he would recall that memorable day as a prelude to many more splendid ones to follow:

> When I got to the room the bellhop opened up the curtains on them big windows and I looked out. I could see almost the whole city. I think it was the palm trees that got me. Every place you looked there was palm trees and it made me feel like I was back in Miami. All of a sudden, I realized for the first time in over 10 years that there was no handcuffs on me and nobody was breathin' over my shoulder, which was the way I used to feel even while I was wanderin' around Italy. When I looked down over the Caribbean from my window, I realized somethin' else; the water was just as pretty as the Bay of Naples, but it was only 90 miles from the United States. That meant I was practically back in America.[3]

The Hotel Nacional in Havana delighted Luciano, and he stayed in room 924. It was a place he desired and missed. It had the obligatory old-style charm and luxury tempered by good taste. The hotel had a little salon for elected officials and an elevator adorned with gilded ironwork for the exclusive use of the president.

In the absence of typical winds, October was dominated by an unbelievably clear sky. December itself presented another challenge, as a month of northern fronts, when it was humid and windy, with waves braking on the rocks supporting the hotel.

Lansky assured Luciano that Fulgencio Batista's "absent presence" still dominated the island. Eleven years in power was too long a time for Batista's influence to be erased. His innumerable public officials still remained, the crowd of politicians who almost all considered themselves enemies of the general when, in reality, they responded to any requirement he might have, however crude. The power groups on the island operated almost in parallel. The power Batista had forged over more than a decade was now mixed and diluted, dispersed among the other leaders comprising the apparent power, whose figurehead was a doctor of physiology. The other (increasingly limited) power belonged to the "invisible heads." For the gangsters, the motto was "all for one," providing there was a confluence of interests.

The meeting in Havana had been called for December 1946, at which time the U.S. Mafia's situation could not have been better. The families had accumulated fabulous fortunes and they had begun to gradually penetrate important areas of the U.S. economy, including the banking system and vital areas of politics. In other words, they had bought, bribed and corrupted to the extent that they acquired great fortunes. Still, they never abandoned their traditional interests, which became apparent with the opening of the empire of Las Vegas. There was also the tourist industry in Florida and various legal investments.

Lansky continued to maintain interests in the south of Florida. There was not a single place in the United States, however, where his operations were as untouchable as they were in Cuba. It was assured, then, that the U.S. Mafia's elite would attend the meeting in Havana. Some 500 people would be there — chiefs and sub-chiefs of the Mafia families, directors, bodyguards, advisers, special guests and more than 100 lawyers tied to big business.

On November 29, 1946, however, the 480 employees of the Hotel Nacional went on strike.[4] They demanded a 30 percent increase in their salaries. Soon, the bars and salons, the kitchen, the garage and the terrace, were all left unattended. Restaurant tables were only partly serviced. There was nobody to clean up, serve drinks or bring cigarettes. The management called on its lawyers to quickly process the case in the courts. Because it was such an important affair, the matter immediately reached the president's office. Grau and his prime minister, Carlos Prío Socarrás, arranged to take serious measures. They summoned the hotel management and strike representatives to the presidential palace. The Hotel Nacional had agreed to a 25 percent raise; but the chefs insisted on 30 percent until, at the final hour, a call from the "invisible heads" to the presidency made known that 30 percent had been granted. The powers-that-be wanted guests and staff to enjoy the greatest harmony that winter.

The Havana meeting took place between December 22 and 26, 1946, and the Hotel Nacional was closed to the public over several days to accommodate their special councils. It was one of the greatest Mafia meetings ever held, presided over by Charles Lucky Luciano, Frank Costello, Vito Genovese, Albert Anastasia, Meyer Lansky and others. During those Christmas holidays, even the ineffable Frank Sinatra traveled to Havana to sing in honor of Luciano, as spheres of influence were reordered, not just in the United States, but in the most important parts of the Caribbean.

The "delegates" did not want caviar, filets, tenderloin or champagne to be brought to their luxurious suites. Rather, they requested exquisite crab or queenconch *enchilados,* brought from the southern archipelago. They called for roast breast of flamingo, tortoise stew, roast tortoise with lemon and garlic, crayfish from Cojímar, oysters from Sagua and grilled swordfish. They developed a taste for the delicious grilled venison chops sent by the minister from Camagüey, who owned livestock, and the succulent mystery that was the flesh of the manatee. They ordered the best aged rum and Montecristo cigars, while Hatuey or Tropical beer was always on the table.

They ate two or three times every night. They drank and argued, or settled important questions; and, at times, at unaccustomed hours, they called at the presidential palace.

Mike Miranda made his presence known at that unlawful assembly. He offered deals involving car agencies, slot machines, racetracks and insurance companies. He had particular experience in controlling labor unions. Another who made his presence known was Joseph Magliocco, greeting others with the greatest of pleasure. Magliocco managed diverse interests related to beverages, import and export companies, chains of laundry establishments and the distribution of olive oil. He also had great influence with labor unions.

Of course, Vito Genovese attended, a man whose interests included race tracks, import and export businesses, advertising agencies, chains of restaurants and bars, in a network that included various activities at the port. Most importantly, at that time Vito aspired to be chief boss of the U.S. Mafia, with the aim of taking total control of the drug traffic. The deals were diverse, complex, interwoven.

Giuseppe Bonanno was there, whose interests revolved around pompous funerals, the clothing industry, import and export houses, laundry chains and the distribution of olive oil and cheese.

It would take too long to list all the interests and deals of each of the *capos* who traveled to Havana at the end of 1946. The principal bosses of the New York clans were there: Joe Adonis, Albert Anastasia and Frank Costello. From New Jersey: Tommy Luchese, Joe Profaci, Willie Moreti and Angie Pisano. From Chicago: Taone Accardo (one of the principal advisers) and the Fischetti brothers, cousins and heirs of Al Capone. It is said that Al Capone sent greetings to his great friend Lucky. Although Capone had been released from jail, he could not attend the meeting because he was confined to one of his Palm Beach mansions, suffering from cerebral syphilis. Also in Havana were Carlos Marcello from New Orleans; Steve Magdino representing the families of Buffalo and old Santo Trafficante Snr. from Florida.

The Mafia made sure that the Hotel Nacional was the most peaceful place in the world. The first floor was prepared for the deliberations of the businessmen. At night, charming parties were held. The Nacional had to be calm, to allow for nightly recreation with women chosen from the payrolls of the Tropicana, Montmartre and Sans Souci, or from the Casas de Marina. It was first-rate for the guests, and nobody felt bothered or threatened during that memorable meeting.

A good number of rooms were reserved in the Presidente, Inglaterra and Sevilla Biltmore hotels for service personnel. Exceptional measures were also taken in the Boyeros airport and other places in the city. The Hotel Nacional closed its doors to all outside interests. Nobody could enter the premises — not journalists, the police or bureaucrats of the Cuban Government.

There were 50 cars with chauffeurs at the ready. A select commission was charged with receiving the guests, taking into account that some, for whatever reason, might arrive late. Access to the hotel was guarded by hand-picked men. Without arousing attention, they watched the gardens, the entrances to the Malecón and paths that led to O Street.

Given the widespread implications of the meeting, and to avoid any risk, everything was anticipated and carefully managed. On December 15, 1946, precisely a week before people began to arrive, National Airlines inaugurated a direct service between Havana and New York.

A cover had to be devised for such a high-level meeting, so a group of Frank Sinatra's admirers made the trip to Havana. An Italian millionaire invited Sinatra, with idea of staging an elaborate homage to the entertainer, in the exquisite salons of the Hotel Nacional. In reference to this, Luciano himself said:

> If anyone had asked, there was an public reason for such a gathering. It was to honor an Italian boy from New Jersey named Frank Sinatra, the crooner who had become the idol of the nation's bobbysox set. He had flown to Havana with his friends the Fischettis to meet his friend Charlie Luciano, and during the holiday week a gala party would be given in his honor. Frank was a good kid and we was all proud of him, the way he made it to the top... He had a job workin' for Tommy Dorsey's band and he was gettin' about 150 bucks a week, but he needed publicity, clothes, and different kinds of special music things, and they all cost quite a bit of money — I think it was about 50 or 60 grand. I okayed the money and it come out of the fund, even though some guys put up a little extra on a personal basis. It all helped him become a big star and he was just showin' his appreciation by comin' down to Havana to say hello to me.[5]

Time magazine carried a description of Sinatra from this time:

> ...the popular conception of a gangster and model in 1929. He has bright, wild eyes, and his movements suggest sprung steel. He talks out of the corner of his mouth. He dresses with a glaring, George Raft kind of snazziness — rich, dark shirts and white-figured ties...

He is an admitted friend of Joe Fischetti, who is prominent in what
is left of the Capone Mob, and he once made himself a lot of trouble by
buddying up to Lucky Luciano in Havana.[6]

Luciano's presence in Havana was truly eventful. Talks were held on
spheres of influence, territorial problems, the issue of the drug trade
and the opening of the empire of Las Vegas, starting with the famous
Hotel Flamingo. After that 1946 meeting, Luciano applied himself
to a life of parties, dances, horse races, romances and wonderful
encounters.

When the meeting was over, everyone left. Lansky went to
Florida, citing personal problems. Not Luciano, however. He had no
intention of distancing himself from Havana. He stayed, surrounded
by a special circle of friends. He abandoned the Hotel Nacional and
moved to the exclusive Miramar neighborhood, just a few blocks
from the private mansion of President Grau San Martín. Luciano's
new refuge was 30th Street. The house, a little more than 100 meters
from 5th Avenue, was truly secure, with exits to a plot of land and
to 3rd Street.

Two weeks later, a group of select Americans living in the
same neighborhood learned of Luciano's presence, and very soon
invitations began to arrive at number 29.

During those days, Luciano was almost completely happy. Havana
was becoming the ideal place for him. Most of the time, he went
about "alone," with just two bodyguards assigned by Neno Pertierra.
One of the gunmen had been a dealer in the Montmartre casino. His
name was Armando Feo, and it was said he was a very good shot,
with nerves of steel and the manners of a gentleman. The other was a
handsome gunman, known by the nickname "Trabuco." He enjoyed
sexual fame and was used by the Mafia to protect their casinos from
undesirable visitors.

Luciano had already met Paco Prío. "One of our best friends,"
said Lansky, with a certain amount of pride, the day the meeting
took place. "He's the prime minister's brother, and without a doubt,
one of the most important politicians."

Luciano, the supreme boss of the U.S. Mafia, would find any
pretext to leave Armando Feo in the residence on 30th Street and,

with his butler at the wheel of his car, visited the Italian Barletta or the Corsican Battisti.

Barletta would come to be one of the most influential people in Cuba. He was the exclusive representative of General Motors in Cuba. Over the years, Barletta's deals, as the great "visible head" of the brotherhood, would branch out into very large investments. He set up a bank and applied himself to legalizing enormous sums of capital. He came to control businesses in the United States and assumed control of important media on the island. At that time, however, when Amadeo met almost daily with Mr. Lucanio, he was nothing more than an object of persecution.

Battisti, the other recipient of Luciano's calls, had always moved in influential circles, and just taken charge of the strongest port bank in Havana. At the same time, Battisti was head of the race track and business manager of the Casino de la Playa.

Luciano continued to receive invitations from rich Americans. They waited for him in the spacious doorways in the grand mansions on Paseo Street, greeting him like an old friend. He was received and led into the plush living rooms, with their polished marble and crystal, into English gardens, while jazz quintets played tastefully to one side.

One afternoon was pleasant, indeed. Luciano was at first surprised, and eventually quite charmed, after being introduced to one of the most beautiful girls at the party. Beverly Paterno had been looking out for the famous Luciano and extended her hand in an elegant gesture. The couple were seated among mutual friends. They chatted and danced until they departed. Miss Paterno was from a refined New York family. The two arranged to meet the next day.

That night, Luciano requested his car for 9 p.m., and left with Armando Feo and two of his bodyguards. He played in the casino of the race track, and at 11 p.m. they left for the Sans Souci. They passed through the entrance with the little red roof, and immediately saw the lights ahead. There was music, voices and talk of a cockfight organized to impress a new arrival. The car went up the gravel driveway as smoothly as Feo could drive, until they stopped beneath the laurels.

The Sans Souci's manager, Miguel Tray, had Luciano come directly to his office for the initial courtesies, as always. A showgirl was offered to keep him company, but Luciano declined the offer. He wanted to be alone, gambling and drinking.

He was in the casino until 2 a.m. Upon leaving, a man stood in his way. Luciano's protectors immediately stood guard. "I thought I recognized you," said the intruder, without introducing himself. It was the U.S. journalist Harry Wallace. "And I was not mistaken. I saw you in Italy, your birthplace; and what a surprise to find you here in one of the most famous places in Havana."

"No," stated Luciano, "I'm not the person you're looking for."

He didn't want to be bothered; he didn't want to hear anything that could injure his dignity; the bodyguards treated Wallace with excessive rudeness, in spite of Luciano's desire for discretion. Wallace was well known in Havana.[7] He wrote a gossip column for the *Post* newspaper, which was published in English and his stories were well received.

With the official protection he enjoyed, Luciano thought he had nothing to fear; his friends were so influential, he should not have felt threatened by something so simple. He shrugged off the meeting with the journalist.

Together, Luciano and Paterno made the rounds of Havana's exciting places. They went to the horse races and ate coconut icecream. They drank, or enjoyed the sun at some nearby beach. They sat on the terraces by the port or walked along the tree-lined promenades in the afternoon. Today, the premiere of a movie; tomorrow, dinner in a fashionable restaurant. At night, they would grace the scintillating cabarets, enjoying the music of drums and the bodies of fire, with rhythms they always found to be so passionate.

But Luciano was attracting too much attention. He should have distanced himself from publicity, but had allowed himself to be swept away by his passions. Miss Paterno even hired a public relations agent,[8] elaborating a chain of rumors and gossip. Photographs were taken in elegant places. Always, the dapper Luciano and distinguished lady. They were seen by the port, against a backdrop of boats and masts, surrounded by whistle blasts, the sound of cars, flashes of light and voices in the street. As they devoured delicious *paella*, seated on the porch of El Templete, the breeze brought a fierce maritime odor and songs from the Negro quarter.

Then Miss Paterno disappeared. She abandoned Havana mysteriously, just as she had arrived. She left only promises in her wake, and the public record of her outings with Luciano. In under a week, the first news began to appear in the United States: the King of the Mob was in Havana.

In his book, *The Mafia*, Frederic Sondern Jr., affirms that Luciano:

> …with his usual foresight and skill, was entrenching himself in Cuban politics. Congressmen, judges, police chiefs came to Signor Lucania's elaborate and carefully organized parties; they and their wives received expensive presents from an always open hand. It looked as though Signor Lucania was on the way to becoming a power in Cuba.[9]

According to Harry J. Anslinger (commissioner of the Bureau of Narcotics of the U.S. Treasury Department), the U.S. police were in no hurry and monitored all of Luciano's movements from Washington.[10]

Reading between the lines, it is undeniable that Vito Genovese had been arranging everything. The fact that Luciano was living in Havana was first only hinted at in rumors. Later, it was confirmed. His exact place of residence was known, as were the networks and contacts of the large drug trade to which he had become devoted. U.S. narcotics agents confirmed that, even before Luciano left for Cuba, they knew of his secret drug routes, thanks to reports telegraphed from Rome.

Luciano was to suffer another serious reversal of fortune, and this was more clearly the result of an underground operation. During those days, "a well-known Broadway and Hollywood star, an old friend of Lucky's, went to Havana to see him."[11] She was coming for rest and recreation, and she stayed in the Hotel Nacional. Where else could a star feel safer?

Clearly the woman wanted to thank Luciano for some favor, and what better way to express her admiration than to fly to Havana? A party was held for a group of very close friends. There was dinner, music and dancing. The evening was so excessive that nobody noticed when dawn arrived.

How did the rumor of the star's visit reach a certain prestigious school in Havana? Some said it was through the press, though this is not likely. Girls from wealthy families studied at this school, which was run by nuns. Within half an hour of finding out, they had planned a reception for the famous star, who in recent months, had captivated the public with one of her movies. How could the school not take advantage of her visit to Havana?

It was quickly arranged. The students ordered flowers from one of the best florists. They arranged a bus for the pupils, and parchment which they would collectively present to the luminary, after the star had received the box of pineapple and mango-flavored candies. A group of 20 students departed, as though on a pilgrimage. They were the best prepared and most communicative of the girls, who would convey their words of joy in perfect English. It was their opportunity to exalt the school's name.

The bus entered the main entrance of the hotel, stopping near the portico. The girls alighted with their bouquet of flowers, not believing how simple it all seemed. Were they expected? No one stopped them in the lobby. They were directed to an elevator and the operator took them to the ninth floor. The elevator door opened. They saw the plush hallway and a diligent bellhop took them to a half-opened door. Directed by a nun,[12] the whirlwind of girls entered the room, where "…it was rather ribald chaos. There were bottles on the floor, lingerie hung from wall brackets and a number of people lay sleeping where they had collapsed."[13]

The girls' departure was even more exciting. After the licentious vision they had witnessed, the girls left shouting and laughing hysterically. It was an absolute scandal: "The sister reported at once to her mother superior, the mother superior to her bishop."[14]

According to the U.S. police, the commissioner of the Bureau of Narcotics had arranged the whole thing: "Two narcotics agents had been dispatched to Havana, and several employees of the Hotel Nacional were temporarily placed on the Treasury Department's payroll — an elevator man and a telephone operator, among others."[15]

In his foreword to *Brotherhood of Evil: The Mafia*, Harry J. Anslinger said that Sondern was the most capable of accurately presenting the history of the Mafia in the United States: "He has, for years, been close to many of us in various fields of law enforcement and been with us in many battles on its behalf. He knows what he is talking about at first hand."[16] The following account is from Sondern:

> They had reason to believe that before leaving Italy, [Luciano] had set up an extensive organization in that country to smuggle narcotics into Cuba, that he would then send to the United States. Anslinger proceeded to play a waiting game, to find out as much as possible about his contacts and method of operation.
>
> The plan was almost wrecked by an incident, which produced one of the more amusing reports in the Bureau's somber files... [A reference to the visit by the girls and the nuns to Luciano's rooms.][17]
>
> Frenzied narcotics agents reported to Washington that there would undoubtedly be publicity, which would ruin all their schemes. Publicity, by almost superhuman effort, was suppressed. Lucky never knew of the early-morning visitation, and the surveillance continued.[18]

Demonstrating an almost proverbial innocence, the report adds that:

> The Cuban press [which had demonstrated its docile nature during a meeting in the Hotel Nacional in December, and which now appeared to have the green light[19]] eventually of course discovered who the wealthy and generous Signor Lucania was and the news was sensational. But the public reaction was not what Commissioner Anslinger expected. No one seemed disturbed by Lucky's presence on the island. Quite the contrary. By this time Anslinger had found out everything he wanted to know, realized that the first big shipments of narcotics via Cuba to the United States had been organized and now wanted the channel blocked.[20]

More than 40 years have passed, and still the matter of Luciano's defeat in Havana lies wrapped in mystery. If we rely on the head of the Narcotics Division of the U.S. Treasury Department, they had "already discovered everything they wanted to know," so it was logical that Luciano's days were numbered. Surely he should have been arrested and tried, and the drug channels destroyed? One might also have expected that, given Luciano's notorious ties to the Mafia families in Havana, the criminal structure of the American Mob in Cuba should have been swept away and its businesses dismantled.

When Luciano convoked the Havana meeting of factions of the U.S. Mafia, he was in a disadvantageous situation. He had few options, because he had been expelled from the United States, without hope of returning. He decided the best he could do was move permanently to the Cuban capital. Given its proximity to the United States, and the favorable situation the island offered for his operations, he may have believed he could continue to exercise control and preserve his hegemony.

On the contrary, it was inevitable that, sooner or later, a powerful rival would displace Luciano, and his influence would gradually decline.

At the start of 1942, Luciano's worst enemy was not the government in Washington, or its intelligence services. His main stumbling block was the growing economic and political influence of other Mafia groups in the United States, headed by Vito Genovese.

When Luciano chose Havana as his base, this move threatened ambitions and provoked fears, releasing forces that helped to remove him from the Cuban capital. The primary objective of Vito Genovese and other Mafia families was to keep Luciano out of the United States and as far away as possible from their interests there.

A second factor was Meyer Lansky and his interests. Lansky was both Luciano's lieutenant and boss of the empire of Havana, and his assistance in any other circumstance would have been of extraordinary value to Lucky. But the fact that Lucky, the chief of the Mafia, was moving permanently to Cuba threatened Lansky's local rule. Opposition to Luciano from other hostile quarters in any case threatened Mafia business interests on the island.

Everything suggests that Lansky contributed secretly and substantially to Luciano's removal. Luciano did not fully understand the situation; at least not immediately. Several years would pass before he realized the tricks to which he had been subjected.

The third player in this drama might have become, in other circumstances, a powerful ally of Luciano: namely, the government in Washington (particularly, the U.S. intelligence services). The strategic result of the alliance between the U.S. Mafia and the U.S. intelligence services must be considered. This alliance had led to Luciano's being freed at the beginning of 1946. Consider also the U.S. Government's recognition of Lucky Luciano's patriotism, loyalty and democratic spirit. It would not have been odd for him to enjoy more tolerance and impunity, like some other *mafiosi*, especially considering the accelerated process of integration, legalization and intermingling of the business interests built on fortunes from organized crime.

When Luciano's presence in Havana was made public, the government in Washington did not repress the Mafia in the United States itself, or dismantle the empire of Havana. Rather, it devoted itself solely to expelling Luciano, confining him once more to Sicily.

Luciano's presence in Cuba had become embarrassing. Lansky was first to confirm that an unfavorable climate was mounting in the United States. Many people in Washington were on the payroll, and now everyone was running a great risk. The casinos could be dismantled. Deals in the nightclubs, the grand cabarets, the drug routes and the traffic of precious stones could all be undermined. Wealthy tourists would become afraid. Everything was threatened: the abortions, popular gambling, the horse races and operation of companies and corporations that were gradually widening their scope. It was likely that the big bank deals would be damaged. Disgrace might reach even further, tainting friends of the government.

Harry J. Anslinger applied more pressure. He stated that the Public Enemy Number One was in Havana, and to avoid problems for the Cuban Government, Washington "would appreciate his being sent back to Italy."[21]

Several days passed, but nothing happened. Anslinger bolstered his position. He issued new declarations to the U.S. press, accompanied this time by a document sent to the Cuban authorities, demanding Luciano's immediate departure.

President Grau San Martín limited his reply to a memorandum, in which he expressed gratitude for the message but did not make any promises. This memorandum — and an interview the minister of the interior, Alfredo Pequeño, held with the U.S. ambassador in Havana — was the only response. According to the Auténtico Party leadership, in spite of Luciano's bad reputation, his presence in Havana was absolutely legal. His papers were in order, and he was not breaking Cuban law.

Anslinger understood the fragility of his actions and requested the personal assistance of President Truman. According to Anslinger, the U.S. police knew everything about the networks and intrigues directed by the Mafia from Havana; and the U.S. president authorized measures he considered appropriate. In spite of Washington's approval, however, the U.S. Narcotics Division stuck to its demand that Dr. Grau San Martín's government expel Luciano from Cuba at once.

According to sources, Grau then held a meeting with an important group of politicians at the presidential palace. Prime Minister Carlos Prío attended, and the president made known his opposition to U.S. interference. Grau San Martín said words to the effect that: If the Cuban Government is free, we should be entitled to issue visas to whomever we see fit.

It was affirmed at this meeting that reports had been submitted by the Cuban secret police to the presidential office, giving assurances that the Italian American millionaire Salvatore Lucania was subject to strict observation, and had been living peacefully in Havana. Though many thought him quarrelsome; according to Grau, there was no legal requirement for him to leave the country, if he continued to behave in a lawful manner.

Luciano, however, became restless. He suspected danger everywhere. What about the deals Vito Genovese had made? How could Luciano account for his present misfortune? He was overwhelmed by doubt. Maybe the *Post* journalist had something to do with it? Perhaps Wallace was in secret negotiations with the Cuban secret police, and his friends were very influential. Lansky, nevertheless, said it was not so. In this country, he said, no policeman is an enemy.

From the beginning, Lansky was in favor of resisting. (At least, that was the position he appeared to take.) Luciano agreed, and the Cuban Government responded according to its own will. "The Luciano issue is of no importance," affirmed a document signed and sealed in the presidential office. Such was the Cuban Government's formal response to new demands received via the U.S. embassy.

Then the U.S. Government announced the island would be submitted to a blockade of pharmaceutical products. No Cuban company could import medical drugs.There could be no purchase or shipment of legal drugs used in medicinal products. Cuba would be subjected to an embargo, until Luciano was deported.

Midnight calls, messages, private conversations and secret meetings followed. Emissaries and correspondence were sent, until the situation blew up to almost the dimensions of a war. The events of February 1947, have been described as follows:

> Cuban President Ramón Grau San Martín was outraged at the "injustice" of the U.S. threat. Dr. José Andreu, the country's director of public health and a signatory to the international convention covering the use of drugs by all nations, not only disputed Anslinger's claim that Luciano was behind an upsurge in illegal narcotics traffic but also asserted that there was "no legal force able to choke off Cuba's supply of legitimate drugs while it complies with the provisions of the agreement." The U.S. actions, he said, were "arbitrary and unjust." But these were only words. For the Cubans, in reality, had little choice but to accede to the threats and demands; the country had no capacity to manufacture the much-needed medicines and was totally dependent on the United States for them.[22]

Frederic Sondern Jr., tells us:

> The Havana authorities demurred. It finally took the combined pressure of the State and Treasury Departments to persuade them that Lucky would be a constant source of embarrassment between the two governments. But it was not until Washington threatened to cut off the shipment of all legitimate medical narcotics that the Cuban Government at last reluctantly took action.[23]

Besides the furious opposition of Grau San Martín, some politicians formed a group, acting in parallel, and secretly, against public opinion.

As its spokesperson, the group chose Indalecio Pertierra, the Liberal congressman. Meetings with all political parties took place in his mansion. Gathering in the same room, old friends with different ideas, were: Paco Prío, Eduardo Suárez Rivas, Miguelito Suárez

Fernández, Germán Álvarez Fuentes, Acosta Rubio, Alonso Pujol and Santiaguito Rey. It was feared that if the matter grew in importance and reached the ears of the most reticent, the issue would be aired in congress.

It did not happen. Lansky was maneuvering behind the scenes, and made a second trip to Daytona Beach at the urging of Luciano, to determine what new plan could be put forward. He returned with two masterly ideas. General Batista was a man of great imagination, and had proposed different plans, not knowing which would be the best.

The first was related to his old private secretary, the discreet Marín, who was now in Caracas managing one of the large casinos. Negotiations could be made with the Venezuelan Government for a visa legalizing Luciano's entrance into that country's capital, via the Dominican Republic. Luciano would be well received, he could count on very good friends, and he would be showing flexibility in the face of Washington's pressure.

The second variation was bolder. They would ask Dr. Grau, in response to the U.S. Government's threat, and by virtue of the powers conferred upon him by the nation, to respond to the blockade of medicines with a refusal by Cuba to send even an ounce of sugar to the United States.

To Luciano that plan seemed unlikely to succeed, and he consulted with lawyer friends. He also heard the advice of Amadeo Barletta and Amleto Battisti, and all were of the opinion that it was an impossible idea. How in the world would Cuba resist?

There was no other way, and he asked Lansky to forget the matter. A day before Luciano was arrested, Batista sent him a message by courier. After hearing the message, Luciano concluded that all was lost. The general, without beating around the bush, had advised Luciano to leave, and wait for better times. But Luciano, overcome by skepticism, was convinced that if he left for Italy, he would never be able to return to the U.S. continent.

The next day, on February 23, 1947, he was arrested in a restaurant in Vedado. Benito Herrera, chief of police in Havana, delegated the operation to one of his lieutenants. The officer conducted himself with extreme courtesy. He asked Luciano if he would please accompany him. It was Saturday, and they could pass by the residence on 30th Street to collect any necessary items.

Luciano did not lose his composure. He too was very courteous. He bade his bodyguards a fond farewell, then left peacefully in the custody of Cuban agents.

Lansky would see him two or three more times, exhibiting all the hypocrisy of which he was capable. Lansky said he was afraid for the security of his deals and networks. He was especially worried about the security of his most valuable men. In reality, however, no other *mafioso* would be persecuted or bothered. In spite of having been arrested, Luciano was not accused or put on trial; and the U.S. Mafia's operative structure in Havana was not touched. The only important thing was that Luciano should leave Cuba. The farce had been staged in a masterly way; and, in a few days, the Cuban drug companies began to receive shipments of legal drugs again, or rather, of raw materials supposedly used in the production of medicines. (The companies had special licenses, authorizing them to receive such shipments, and they drew on it many times throughout the year.)

The March 1947 events in which Lucky Luciano played the main role did not represent any attempted repression of the U.S. Mafia's activities in Cuba. On the contrary, deals reached greater heights, as did the impunity with which they were made. Over the years, the deals multiplied, proving that the only obstruction to them had been Luciano.

Even today, many claim that Luciano's departure from Cuba was owing to Washington's pressure and demands. Nothing is further from the truth. The U.S. Government was only the apparent power. Pressure was applied, and demands were made, but they were manipulated demands, and did not emanate from the intentions of the U.S. Government toward the Cuban nation. Rather, Washington's demands were a response to power struggles between the Mafia families. All the players in this game wanted Luciano to leave Havana, both the powerful Mafia interests in New York on one side and the treacherous boss of the empire of Havana on the other.

As for his part in the affair, Harry J. Anslinger's attitude was strictly professional.

The rancor of Vito Genovese was different. If Luciano returned to the United States, Genovese could say goodbye to his own claim on Mafia supremacy. Lansky's attitude was simpler. For him, as long as Lucky remained in Cuba, the empire Lansky had constructed would not be entirely his. He would have to share it with someone of higher rank. Luciano was his boss — and, besides that, a Sicilian. Lansky had no reason to protect Luciano, and events unfolded very quickly. An inflexible law was being obeyed. When the enemies' interests coincided with friends' desires, there was nothing else to do. There were two great forces against Luciano — two forces that, at the end of the next decade, would lead to a brutal war to divide up Cuba.

On March 29, 1947, Charlie Lucky Luciano abandoned the island aboard a Turkish freighter. He traveled first class, and his departure was an event of some note. It was chronicled in the radio reports transmitted by Eduardo R. Chibás every Sunday.

Many important people would trouble themselves to see him off, and Lucanio responded with those saintly manners of his. He was courteous, even friendly, and resplendent. Of all the embraces he received, none was as warm and strong as that from Paco Prío, older brother of the future president.

Batista's Return

Toward the end of 1946, important meetings had been taking place in the residence of ex-President Batista.

Grau, for his part, had designs on reelection. Meanwhile, the poorest sectors had to withstand huge unemployment and the black market. The poor also had to put up with systematic robbery by the Auténtico Party. It was during this period that the gangsters of Cuban politics began carrying out McCarthy-like repression. Repression of communists, progressive intellectuals and the labor and peasant movements was particularly intense, and aimed at preventing a unification of these forces.

The Mafia and the intelligence apparatus of the United States were behind these moves to confront, divide and eradicate revolutionary influence. A preferred method was the murder of the most important leaders of the popular movements.

The imperialists feared that, at some moment, an insurrection would mobilize the oppressed majority of Cuban society. The intelligence agencies and the Mafia agreed that the Grauist group's hold on power was rather temporary.

In reality, the group's rise was accompanied by too many compromises. These made it difficult for Grau to explain his party's alliances with supporters of Machado and Batista, such as Aquilino Lombard and Guillermo Alonso Pujol.

Of all the political arrangements into which Grau was forced, none was as incomprehensible to public opinion as the compromise he made with a man who would occupy the vice-presidency. Brought in from outside the Auténtico Party, Dr. Gustavo Cuervo Rubio was known as a fierce conservative. In 1922, Cuervo had published a book denying the existence of U.S. imperialism, in addition to justifying the politics of intervention carried out by the United States in Cuba. He was a partisan of the Platt Amendment, and his ideas did not correspond with the political program that the Auténtico Party leadership advocated when it was called upon to form government.

In 1944, Grau assembled his cabinet. He designated as prime minister the habitually indolent Dr. Félix Lancís y Sánchez,[1] who was fond of high appointments requiring little work. Another minister was Dr. Segundo Curti, the son of Italians living in Havana. In one admiring gesture, Curti declared that Grau San Martín was the best president in the history of Cuba. Dr. Curti would be his minister of the interior.

The office of minister of agriculture fell to a man from Camagüey who was the owner of drug companies, ranches and other businesses, Dr. Álvarez Fuentes. He was sponsor, in the international airport of Camagüey, of the flights of Aerovías Q. His drug company was in the center of Camagüey, but his successes transcended the borders of the Caribbean.

To the amazement of all, Batista's vice-president, Dr. Gustavo Cuervo Rubio, was charged with the Ministry of State in the new government. On the evening of October 10, 1944, after the assignment of duties in the presidential palace, many embraces, conciliatory whispers and smiles for the press, Cuervo took possession of his new appointment, which until that moment had been occupied by Jorge Mañach, of the pro-fascist group ABC.

Another spectacular appointment was the Ministry of Communications to Mosquito Clark. This lucky man, according to the press of the day, was neither a consummate politician, an apparent "revolutionary," nor a person of great charisma. He did not have political influence or social contacts. Furthermore, he had no experience in power struggles. He had simply lived in the area of Las Tunas as an employee of a sugar company, and his appointment seemed strange to everyone. He was not rich, and lived far from the capital. He was completely unfamiliar with those realms in which Cuban destinies were apparently decided.

The minister of communications was a ham radio enthusiast. He devoted many hours to this activity. Clark was also a confidant of the Manatí sugar refinery, and spent days at a table with his apparatus, transmitting and receiving messages. It was during Machado's fall that Clark proved he was useful. Laborers were occupying the sugar refineries, groups were forming and our protagonist observed that the workers were getting ready to occupy the Rionda family's sugar refinery. Because he was worried about the situation, it occurred to Clark to use his ham radio knowledge and he began transmitting in English — to the U.S. fleet that surrounded the island — so the U.S. Marines were able to act decisively.

Thanks to the many transformations of the Auténtico Party, General Batista's new political thrust was quite advanced by 1948. The process began on October 10, 1944, the very day of his exile to Daytona Beach — he stayed there four years, one month and nine days — during which time he took care of the affairs of Cuba, waiting to be called on in a time of great need. Batista's house was a beautiful chalet, surrounded by trees and flowers in one of Florida's most exclusive areas. Beside the English garden, the peaceful Halifax River flowed behind his estate, connected to it by a little pier.

A dozen bodyguards protected Batista in the United States, not counting the special services afforded him by the country.

For normal business, Batista met visitors in the house. For matters of protocol or friendship, he met them in the English garden. Very discreet meetings took place on the river, in the boat, when dusk had fallen, with the lights of Beach Street Boulevard in the distance.

Batista opted for a more casual dress code in Miami. Visitors did not have to observe the protocol that prevailed during his rule in Cuba — when one could not visit the general without a suit and tie. The days of Batista's dispute with Pedraza had been left behind.

the most scintillating hotel chain of the Caribbean. Between 1947 and 1948, however, it would be unfair to attribute to Suárez Rivas the prosecution of the most important operations and maneuvers that enabled Batista's return. The principals in these arrangements were Carlos Prío and Guillermo Alonso Pujol and, in particular, a celebrated person who during the Auténtico Party rule occupied the presidency of the senate: Dr. Miguel Suárez Fernández.

Much earlier, in September 1947, Prío had made a promise: if he won power, he would permit Batista to return, with all the prerogatives and guarantees that an ex-president deserved.[3] According to documents of the period, this message was transmitted to Batista by Guillermo Alonso Pujol, Prío's vice-president.[4]

The plan was for Batista to return as a senator, so he could enjoy parliamentary immunity against any contingency. We must point out, however, that by 1948 Batista did not have the least possibility of being elected, not from Las Villas or from any other province. The people had repudiated Batista. In addition, the Auténtico Party dominated the Las Villas region. The Auténtico Party maintained the senatorial majority in that province, and the Batista option was impossible.

The Auténtico Party and Miguel Suárez Fernández, its chief representative in Las Villas, went into a complete retreat. They did not organize the election in Las Villas, renouncing the senatorial majority of that province. The objective was for Batista to have every possibility of gaining political power and of mounting an intense campaign at a cost of millions.[5] The Auténtico Party (with Senator Miguel Suárez Fernández at the head) permitted Batista's certificate of election to reach the number of votes required.

It was customary for important Cuban politicians to disappear from Havana, on brief discreet trips to the south of the United States. Sailing with the Gulf Stream on a private yacht, Florida could be reached in a few hours, though most of these people preferred the special flights of the Aerovías Q airline. Other, more innocent, airlines also flew daily from Havana to Chicago, stopping in Houston, where the travelers could readjust their itineraries. The Douglas planes of Expreso Interamericano were also efficient. They made three or four stops: Miami; Vero Beach; some other point on the Florida peninsula; before landing at Daytona Beach. The list of people is long who, at that time, traveled secretly to hold audience with Batista: ex-military men, old and new politicians, businessmen, gunmen, policemen, professional players, secret agents and some *mafiosi*.

On various occasions, José Manuel Alemán, Grau's minister of education, left the Cuban capital for a brief time. (Alemán was charged with paying the gangster groups.) It is known that on at least one occasion he was accompanied by Rolando Masferrer (one of the chief gunmen in the service of the politicians of the apparent power). Together they went to address matters of great importance.

The ex-presidential candidate Carlos Saladrigas also went to Florida several times. His meetings with Batista in Daytona were extremely warm. Other people organized trips that turned out to be more torturous. The Catalan Eusebio Mujal Barniol, who directed the Auténtico Party workers' front — he and Masferrer were closely tied to the U.S. intelligence services — traveled to meet Batista. The ex-General Tabernilla made discreet trips. What had been discussed during Tabernilla's visits was communicated rapidly to a group of retired military men.

Julio Lobo made the crossing, allegedly for reasons of health. Alonso Pujol and Santiaguito Rey left Cuba each time some important event occurred. Paco Prío made the trip, too, carrying the best wishes of his brother. Every so often, the ex-Major Mariano Faget passed by to express his loyalty and respect. Visits from Congressman Indalecio Pertierra were customary. The García Montes brothers also traveled to Daytona, especially the lawyer and consultant for the Chase Manhattan Bank. In addition, Mr. Martínez Sáenz (otherwise known as José Manuel Martínez Zaldo), who held a key person in the operations of the Barletta family, would also pay his respects.

Of the Mafia families established in Havana, only Santo Trafficante Snr. could approach Batista; Barletta measured his movements, now that he was beginning to organize new important business deals with the aid of the Prío family. In general, Batista's affairs were managed directly by Lansky, in spite of the fact that the chief of the empire of Havana had resettled in the United States. Both men could quickly travel to New York, although the usual thing was for Lansky to pass through Florida every so often, so they could converse in complete tranquility. But of all the travelers, the one who behaved with most caution was the Auténtico's Miguel Suárez Fernández, president of the senate of the republic.

Seen in a historical dimension, these multiple contacts between Batista and the most important figures in the Auténtico Party leadership were impressive. (We must also remember that the Mafia and the U.S. secret police protected Batista). The meetings took place not only in Batista's residence (before 1948), but also in room 726 of the luxurious Martinique Hotel in Miami Beach (after 1950). Here, Auténtico Party politicians and supporters of Batista arrived secretly, to advise him on many complex issues faced by the Auténtico Party.

Batista and the movement's leaders sustained a constant exchange of opinions, criteria, ideas and appraisals of the Cuban political scene. (During his 11 years in power, Batista had permitted the organization of a crime apparatus, at the service of the American Mob. It had gained such power that, at any moment, he could always be called upon to reassume power.) Some "double agents" — such as Santiaguito Rey Pernas or Eduardo Suárez Rivas — had liaisons with U.S. intelligence and the U.S. Mafia and would soon carry out missions within or very close to the Auténtico Party leadership.

As part of these interrelationships, Dr. Fernando Sirgo was included in the propaganda commission directing the electoral campaign of Dr. Carlos Prío Socarrás. Dr. Sirgo was an old friend of Batista's and an efficient secretary in Batista's office.[2]

It must be pointed out that, by 1946, the Auténtico Party had lost all prestige, and the power exercised by its leadership was in

complete chaos. It was only of continuing use to the imperialists, as a tool through which they could advance their interests: namely, the ferocious persecution of communists and the domination and repression of the Cuban labor movement.

By that time, Batista's personal ambitions coincided with the future interests of the financial-Mafia-intelligence service groups. He knew that he once more represented an option for power. He prepared for his return. At first, he alleged that it would not be to participate in politics, but to found a newspaper. The man in charge of creating this cover was Eduardo Suárez Rivas. The story would be fabricated, and circulated by the press.

But for Batista to return, not a few arrangements had to be made. He would have to avoid, among other inconveniences, a hearing on Court Case Number 30, of 1943. The case was pending in the First Criminal Court of the City of Havana. It had been brought because of Batista's various improprieties, fraudulent activities and abuses involving dredging operations carried out at Cárdenas and Isabela de Sagua and for the so-called improvement of the beach at Varadero.

At the same time secret trips were being made by Alonso Pujol, Batista denied that he was planning a comeback from Florida. He contradicted himself, pretended to be uncertain, and behaved in such a way as to convince people that what he was doing (or would do) was spontaneous rather than calculated.

In Daytona, Batista had frequent conversations with the president of the Liberal Party, Senator Suárez Rivas (from Las Villas). Rivas had served as a front man for Luciano, so the latter could establish himself in Cuba. Rivas had participated in the most famous dispute between the Auténtico Party and the Truman Government; the gambling activities of his nephew were notorious. Later, Rivas was minister of agriculture during the Prio Government; and by 1950-51, had managed to project his name as a future president, backed by the Auténtico Party coalition. Later, after 1952, he helped Batista reorganize the criminal state. Finally, he wound up as secretary of the Compañía Hoteles La Riviera de Cuba (a front company) used by the "Mafia financier," Lansky. This company was involved with far-reaching projects, the grand purpose of which was to convert Havana into a showcase for

The Kefauver Commission and the Decline of Eduardo Chibás

Creole gangsterism, McCarthy-like in nature, constituted in Cuba an efficient means of corruption to be used against the old Communist Party and the vigorous workers' movement directed by Lázaro Peña. This culture of corruption was heightened by various base motives: personal interests, the settling of accounts and vendettas, and played itself out in executions and innumerable other criminal activities.

Dr. Carlos Prío Socarrás was initially from the Ministry of Labor, and later became prime minister. Organized gangsterism made it possible for him to slip into the presidency of the republic for a second time during the Auténtico Party period, along with a vice-president who was tied completely to the political-military leadership of General Batista.

In a report submitted to the exchequer, published also in the press of the day, the young lawyer Fidel Castro denounced President Prío for his close ties to gangsterism:

> Prío is no stranger when it comes to dealings with gangs. They guarded him jealously throughout his entire political campaign. He rose to power soaked in compromise... Aside from giving jobs to other smaller groups, he gave 60 government posts to Guillermo Comellas's group. He gave 110 to the Tribunal Ejemplar Revolucionario; 120 to the Unión Insurreccional

Revolucionaria; 150 to Acción Guiteras; 400 to Colorado's group and he gave 500 to Masferrer's group. To Policarpo's group, which was the most fearful, he gave 600 posts. According to data in my hands, this makes a total of 2,120 jobs that were assigned without extra services being assigned to the ministries of Public Health, Labor, Interior and Public Works. The number of government posts per person in some cases is alarming: for example, Manuel Villa has 30, Guillermo "El Flaco" has 28, Pepe "El Primo" has 26, the "Boxer" (I do not know his name) has 26, listed on the payrolls under different workers' names...

The pistols that kill are paid for by Prío.

The cars with which the killings take place are paid for by Prío.

The men that kill are supported by Prío.[1]

Resources to support gangsterism were obtained by means of the famous "Clause K" account. About 3.4 million pesos (equal to the dollar) were invested each month to support and finance these groups. By October 1948, the "Clause K" account had an overdraft of 11 million pesos, accumulated during the previous 10 months.[2]

The Prío family, besides being friends of the most important U.S. Mafia families, quickly became enthusiastic about the use of cocaine. They were a clan that exemplified the delirious period of the formation of the criminal state during its second stage (1944-52).

By the first months of 1948, cocaine could be bought in Chicago for US$16 per 100 pounds and sold in Cuba for US$65. From this business, 5,000 pesos were taken to the third floor of the presidential palace every day. The fraudulent practices of the Corporation Council (purchasing abroad) also ran into the millions, while in the antituberculosis clinics of the country there was not a single gram of streptomycin. Embezzlement in the Customs House of Havana rose to seven million pesos, and tens of millions were set aside to cover the conversion of the dollar and the buying of gold. The fiscal regions of the country were defrauded of millions. The Treasury also committed frauds worth several millions. By skimming from the taxes that were collected, the palace found 60,000 pesos per day. The National Lottery took two pesos for every ticket sold which, multiplied by 43,000 tickets, equaled 80,000 pesos per week.[3]

The Auténtico Party period was characterized by scandal, robbery, fraud and corruption.[4] During the Auténtico Party regime, administrative corruption became generalized. Speculation, fraudulent deals, low salaries and spiraling inflation were rife. Grau and Prío accentuated the corruption to the point of delirium. Essentially, the crisis in the Auténtico Party was a result of the boundless ambition of its leadership. Clearly, the highest-ranking Auténtico Party politicians had always felt part of a fleeting political moment, as a force at the service of the financial-Mafia-intelligence services groups of the United States. Consequently, they had to act fast.

An analysis of the previous period (1934-44) reveals another aspect of their situation. Batista had held the majority in the 1930s. He was a faithful representative of the forces operating against the interests of the Cuban nation. More significantly, the ex-sergeant had created solid foundations to insure a rigorous historical continuity throughout his period.

Batista had always maintained control within the apparent power, but the Auténtico Party politicians did not have even that. The forces that began to dominate the Cuban economy and its politics granted Batista a certain participation in controlled business deals. Batista, however, was an extraordinarily guarded man. In spite of having become a millionaire, the general never made large investments within the country, unless secretly, in operations related to Mafia interests.

Only the swindles and robberies that depended completely on the administration were reserved for the Auténtico Party leadership, while the juiciest deals remained off-limits. Thus, the U.S. Government's reaction was explainable, when Prío tried to exceed certain bounds by becoming involved with deals reserved exclusively for the dominant power groups.[5]

Two events hastened secret arrangements being made by the U.S. financial-Mafia-intelligence services group, leading to the coup d'état of 1952. The first was a moral campaign led by Eduardo R. Chibás, the other was the scandal produced in the United States by revelations of the Kefauver Commission.[6]

By March 1950, Tennessee Senator Estes Kefauver had completed an extensive investigation into organized crime in the principal U.S.

cities, reaching the conclusion that the Mafia in the United States comprised an outrageous conspiracy.[7] The Kefauver Commission presented a list that included the most important *capos* of the U.S. underworld. These *mafiosi* had succeeded in creating veritable empires, not just in terms of illicit businesses, but in important and numerous legitimate companies.

The cities most affected by this trinity of interests — crime, business and politics — were Miami, Tampa, New Orleans, St. Louis, Detroit, Los Angeles, San Francisco, Las Vegas, Philadelphia, Washington, Chicago and New York.

Senator Kefauver headed the investigation, pointing out key factors that characterized the Mafia's expansion in the United States:

1. A nationwide crime syndicate does exist in the United States of America, despite the protestations of a strangely assorted company of criminals, self-serving politicians, plain blind fools, and others who may be honestly misguided...

2. Behind the local mobs that make up the national crime syndicate is a shadowy, international criminal organization known as the Mafia, so fantastic that most U.S. citizens find it hard to believe it really exists...

5. Infiltration of legitimate business by known hoodlums has progressed to an alarming extent in the United States. The committee uncovered several hundred instances where known hoodlums, many of them employing the "muscle" methods of their trade, had infiltrated more than 70 types of legitimate businesses.[8]

The commission also revealed that, since 1942, arrangements had been made to expand drug channels, "to bring heroin from Marseilles via Cuba to Kansas City for distribution in the Midwest."[9]

For eight days in March 1951, the commission held a series of public hearings in New York. The top racketeers of the United States were subpoenaed.[10] They were seated and interrogated in front of television cameras. The existence of the Mafia was questioned very seriously. For the first time, television was used to expose organized crime in the United States. Transmitted to the entire country, it permitted tens of millions of U.S. citizens to confront the shocking reality of what had been going on.

The entire nation trembled, and it must be presumed that the Mafia felt truly threatened. Several of the great names — Joe Adonis, Frank Costello, Vito Genovese, Umberto Anastasio, Meyer Lansky, Joe Profaci and other famous Mobsters — must have shivered for the first time, as their interests were placed in grave danger. They were a wealthy elite which had achieved great prominence, and were at the time overseeing the legalization of their multi-million dollar fortunes.

The Kefauver Commission showed that the Mafia was still vulnerable in 1950 — despite arrangements to integrate Mob interests with the wider economic and political structures of the United States.

But the Kefauver revelations were gradually covered up, through those very arrangements between power groups in the United States. As Sondern Jr. comments: "...the total accomplishment of the Kefauver Committee has never really been totted up for the public to see."[11] Its impact was diluted, little by little, through a process that was manipulated from the highest levels and would lead, in 1963, to the assassination of President John F. Kennedy.

In mid-1951, however, the Mafia had good reason to feel its interests were under threat. Danger also surrounded the groups that had settled in Havana since 1934, when Luciano reorganized more than 100 groups and Meyer Lansky took charge of Florida and areas of the Caribbean, including Cuba.

After Kefauver Commission revelations rocked the United States, however, the Havana groups were in the best position to organize a rear guard that would assure them impunity.

Two factors in 1950-51 posed perceived dangers for the Havana Mafia — pressure faced by the Mafia in the United States, and a local attempt to institute morality and decency, as epitomized by Eduardo R. Chibás.

Chibás led a dissident wing of the Auténtico Party ranks. His moral crusade, in reality, posed a more immediate threat to Mafia businesses in Cuba than did the exposure of rival gangs in the United States.

Although traditional politicians, opportunists, secret agents and large landowners had penetrated the leadership of Chibás's party, it had by 1951 attracted the dissatisfied majority, who demanded a government capable of combating widespread government corruption.

Other forces trying to resist the maneuvers of the U.S. financial-Mafia-intelligence groups had been persecuted and repressed for years. The labor unions and the revolutionary left had been dislodged from the formerly powerful Cuban labor movement, which was in the hands of Eusebio Mujal. Similarly, a campaign of defamation had been unleashed against the old Communist Party. Aided by this campaign, the assassination of prestigious leaders proceeded, among them Jesús Menéndez of the sugar producers and Aracelio Iglesias of the port workers of Havana. The peasant movements in Camagüey and Oriente were also persecuted, and some prominent leaders assassinated.

By 1951, the U.S. intelligence services considered that leftist forces in Cuba — given the intense repression to which they had been subjected — were incapable of mounting effective resistance on the island.

The mass media in Cuba — radio, television and print — were used to manipulate political events and were extraordinarily successful, constituting a veritable power base in themselves. Besides the traditional Cuban press, other important consortia sprung up that was dependent on the diverse political-military leadership, such as that run by the Goar Mestre brothers.

The Mafia, for its part, looking for greater influence in that complex and precarious balance, also began to operate its own media, such as in the newspaper *El Mundo,* the radio station Unión Radio and some television channels.

In spite of everything, it appeared that Chibás would become the next president. Although his political program did not offer profound economic and social transformations, it did stress the urgent need for the administrative, moral and political reform of the country. Given the situation in Cuba, his agenda did not corresponded in no way to the scheme imposed in Cuba by U.S. imperialism.

The following is part of a letter sent, on December 31, 1950, by Orestes Ferrara (a corrupt politician of Italian origin) to Guillermo

Alonso Pujol, who was the vice-president of Cuba, in the government of Carlos Prío Socarrás:

> You will tell me [wrote Ferrara from Naples] that I consider Chibás is already occupying the presidency. No. From a distance, I cannot give such precise opinions. But the elections should be honored and are beyond appeal, for which reason one must consider well, beforehand, what one is doing... In the situation in Cuba, Chibás must be carried down a constructive path, one of tranquility and without stridency. Otherwise, a situation must be presented that is oriented toward the same ends of honor and public decency, removing the exclusivity from a program that, after all, is an aspiration of all good citizens, not of one party or another... If I have spoken of this before, it is because I consider it a crucial problem. My synthesis is this: if the manifest popular will is that Chibás be president, you must see that he reaches power as a man of the state and not with the attitude of a demagogue. If this is not possible, you must manage to dissuade public opinion, presenting candidates and programs that make the ideas of this rising leader ineffective...
>
> Since Chibás will lead the government merely because of his name (because he is the party), it becomes more important than in other situations to know his thinking beforehand.[12]

The letter was extremely private. At the time it was sent, Lucky Luciano was also in Naples.[13] But Pujol published it immediately, with the intention of preventing others from doing so first; because, by then, Pujol was making secret contacts with General Batista regarding the coup d'état.[14]

Chibás was then submitted to a process of severe psychological vexation, which would lead him, eventually, to suicide.

Analysis of events leads us to believe that U.S. intelligence mounted a covert operation to eliminate Chibás. As a vehicle for psychological manipulation, they employed President Prío's minister of education, Aureliano Sánchez Arango. Chibás became embroiled in accusations concerning a certain contraband coffee scandal. The level of tension and demoralization was such that, in the face of public demand, President Prío declared he could not:

> ...allow the army to be attacked in that way, with the denunciations that you are formulating! You have no right to concentrate your attacks on

Columbia [the country's principal military camp] when the contraband phenomenon also occurs in other airports. Only 20 percent of the illegal commerce is carried out through the camp at Columbia.[15]

Aureliano's first move in this anti-Chibás operation was to direct insinuations at the leader of the Ortodoxo Party. He accused Chibás of having been compromised, by taking part in the tainted coffee speculation. As usual, Chibás took the false accusation as a matter of personal honor.

The atmosphere was clouded by certain mysterious trips that President Prío, without the authorization of congress, was making to Guatemala in Aureliano's private plane — a preamble to a new act of villainy.

Chibás was also waging a general battle against the corruption of the Auténtico Party government. Of the many felonies committed daily by the Auténtico Party, Chibás singled out a supposedly fraudulent operation in Guatemala for denunciation. He accused Aureliano of using breakfast money for school children to buy parcels of land in Guatemala, for the construction of a luxurious real estate developments. Aureliano counterattacked immediately, calling Chibás a liar and demanding proof. Chibás promised to produce evidence of the fraud, which, according to him, was to be found in his very own briefcase. From here on, the invisible powers handled the whole affair.

The Chibás-Aureliano controversy was soon converted into the focus of national interest, in a process that led to a public confrontation on television. Public hysteria was whipped up by the masterly manipulation of radio ads, newspaper columns, rumor and gossip. All other matters were ignored, as everyone waited for Chibás to open his famous briefcase.

For the debate to take place, a long list of conditions was imposed upon Chibás by Aureliano, who accepted them one by one. The first condition was that the debate should last four days. This was unusual, but Chibás accepted. The next condition was that Chibás could not accuse the president of the republic in any of his digressions, or otherwise discuss him. This was more than unusual, but Chibás accepted the condition.

The matter of the real estate development in Guatemala had become something of an obsession for Chibás, and Aureliano imposed another condition: there could be no allusion to Prío's government. The debate should concentrate only on his (Aureliano's) supposed investment in real estate in Guatemala.

The encounter was set for July 21, 1951, at 9:30 p.m., in the assembly chamber of the Ministry of Education. Television and radio would cover the event. Chibás was to arrive alone, with the briefcase and evidence in hand. Chibás was confident he could win. He also believed, or had been made to believe, he had the necessary proof. Perhaps someone he trusted promised him proof of the Guatemalan real estate project.

In a radio broadcast, Chibás announced that he would present the awaited proof. (By this stage, he no longer had access to television.) When he spoke on July 29, he knew he had been deceived.

In this next-to-last address, he did not belabor the Guatemalan real estate issue. Rather, he returned to his impassioned, well-informed and biting criticism. He attacked the Auténtico Party leadership for its corrupt behavior. He also denounced the real business of Aureliano with the Prío family in Guatemala: the exploitation of a giant lumber consortium.

But it was already too late. Public opinion had been conditioned. In scarcely three weeks, Aureliano and his allies had turned the vast tide of opinion. People were no longer interested in any new accusations Chibás could demonstrate to be true. They only wanted proof of the presidential real estate development project in Guatemala. This is how *Bohemia* magazine dealt with the matter: "In reality, the Sunday address from Chibás was far from what the entire population was anxiously expecting. The citizenry came away defrauded after the hour-long speech. Even Chibás's tone of voice was different that night."[16]

As part of the plan, threats had been tossed about. It was rumored that the debate would not be covered by the press or transmitted by television, and Chibás even feared the debate would not take place.

He feared the confrontation could be suspended or evaded by the leadership of the Auténtico Party. Consequently, on July 21, he sent a letter to Aureliano, offering new concessions:

> I accept beforehand and without discussion all the new conditions that you have formulated and that you may formulate in the future, until 9:30 p.m. tonight. I accept that the subject to be dealt with should be the one you indicate: "Parcels of land in Guatemala and misappropriation of school children's breakfast money and material." I accept also that the subject be exclusively "Guatemala," eliminating the other two matters. I accept from the beginning any other variant you propose. I accept what you want in order to avoid the suspension of the debate. I demand only one thing: absolute freedom of speech.[17]

A conspiracy was in progress. Aureliano held secret meetings with the Ministry of the Presidency and the chief of the national police, with the Prío family and legal advisers.

The letter that the leader of the Ortodoxo Party received at the last moment is evidence of the psychological manipulation to which Chibás was being subjected:

> It has cost me time and patience, but at last I have you in the appropriate venue, from which you have made great attempts to escape. I await you, then, tonight in the assembly chamber of the Ministry of Education to debate, exclusively, these three subjects, which are interrelated: your dishonorable slander that I am promoting a residential real estate project in Guatemala with funds from the misappropriation of school breakfast money.
>
>   I await you for this, and only for this. When through your habitual methods — which I know better than anyone in Cuba — you depart from the subject, the moderator will warn you. When you repeat your simple scheme — which is without a doubt why you are coming to the assembly chamber — your power to speak will be taken from you definitively. I know your plan — for 24 years I have been aware of your baseness, your pretensions and your acrobatic maneuvers, all dishonorable and based on bad faith, your strident hysteria — I know, and I repeat to you, that you plan not to fulfill these conditions and not to respect the authority of the moderator.

One last thing: the only one who has understood your famous little paragraph about freedom of speech has been myself. Freedom of speech for you means specifically freedom to insult President Prío, his family and his government, and on the other hand, freedom for you to escape, to flee from your cowardly slander... thus ignoring and forgetting the single topic of the school material and breakfast money related to the real estate in Guatemala.[18]

Aureliano designated as moderator of the debate Octavio de la Saurée Tirapó, director of the Journalism School of Havana, parliamentary chronicler for 20 years, and a man who jealously held on to his post.

That evening, the invisible powers found Chibás in a Vedado restaurant, with Pardo Llada and other friends. Saurée Tirapó went to Chibás's table and gave him the last demands, which required that he make no reference to people in the government, except to the Ministry of Education itself.

Chibás knew it was not possible to touch the subject of Guatemala as a marginal note to other misdeeds of the Auténtico Party, but he accepted. What is more, Chibás agreed not to mention the principal accomplice himself: the president of the republic.

At nightfall, on July 21, police personnel under orders from Major Casals blocked the streets leading to the Ministry of Education. A little before 9 p.m., Chibás appeared. He was alone — his closest collaborators had remained behind. Before Chibás could enter, someone ordered that the door of the assembly chamber of the Ministry of Education be shut. A legion of ushers, bureaucrats and policemen rushed to close it, right in his face.

"You have nothing to do here," a police captain spat at him.

Chibás argued, but it was useless. They did not let him enter, and he had to retire. Meanwhile, Aureliano stood in front of the television cameras and microphones of the numerous radio stations, looking at his watch "as if to give the impression that he was waiting for his adversary."[19]

Then this great pretender assumed center stage. He offered greetings and received applause. The real reason Chibás was absent from the chamber — Aureliano's act of force — was not made public.

Rather, through the lens of manipulated public opinion, it was perceived as impotence and cowardice on the part of the leader of the Ortodoxo Party.

The result was inevitable: the prestige Chibás's had once enjoyed was substantially eroded in the eyes of the public. Chibás was taunted and then simply barred from the assembly chamber.

Chibás committed, in general, two great errors: 1) He changed the method he had been using to denounce the administrative corruption of the Auténtico Party. 2) He offered evidence that he did not have, and which, moreover, it was not necessary for him to present.

The Ortodoxo Party leadership was incapable of protecting Chibás from the intrigue. The leader of the Ortodoxo Party was dragged into a farce conducted behind closed doors, staged in a chamber he was never allowed to enter. These mistakes allowed the intelligence agencies to carry out their project to its conclusion.

The magnates of the Cuban press, who had at first encouraged Chibás — the magazine *Bohemia* and the consortium ruled by the Goar Mestre family had until the "debate" been sympathetic to his moral campaigns — rapidly distanced themselves.

It is interesting to observe how Gaspar Pumarejo (tied to Mafia interests) made concerted efforts — via the national broadcasting Unión Radio station and Unión Televisión channel — to strip the Ortodoxo Party of this powerful means of communication. At the time, all the important maneuvers seemed orchestrated by the Prío family. This, however, was not entirely true. The Barletta family was behind the operation to rob the Ortodoxo Party of television exposure, using the Humara y Lastra company, among others, as a front for their dealings with the national Unión Radio y Televisión.

Pardo Llada worked as director of a popular program called "La Palabra" (The Word). He was one of the first to announce that the Unión Radio y Televisión affair was organized by the Prío family. He did not even wait to be fired, but collected 4,000 pesos for two months' salary and immediately resigned from the program. In those days Pardo Llada was apparently very restless, visibly nervous, up until the very day that Chibás decided to shoot himself.

Chibás was alone. He was cornered. He was threatened with expulsion from congress. His enemies there were about to accuse him of assaulting the stability of national institutions, to deny him parliamentary immunity. In a few days, he had lost his credibility. In a final gesture of integrity, he opted for death, after making a last dramatic appeal to the Cuban people.

After his death, a journalist dared to write an article entitled "He Must Fulfill His Historic Destiny":

> Chibás's adversaries understood, as in gangster movies, that the prosecutor had to be silenced. He could not be bought, and eliminating him physically would have dangerous political consequences. They had to resort to indirect methods.[20]

Long before, President Carlos Prío had outlined the outcome of these events in a message to General Batista, sent via Vice-President Guillermo Alonso Pujol:

> No person who is a friend of mine could undertake the enterprise of making an attempt on the life of Batista... Whoever might be involved in those plans would cease to be my friend immediately, and the full weight of the law would fall upon him. It is clear that an attack on the life of Batista would make Chibás president, just as any aggression against Chibás would make Batista president.[21]

At the Service of the Mafia 6

In 1951, the following political forces were in play in Cuba:

1) The apparent power, installed as the government. This force owed its existence to unbridled corruption, as the three Prío Socarrás brothers tried to ensure continuity for the Auténtico Party (in alliances with the Liberal, Democratic and Republican parties). They were surrounded by people vying for position or carrying out covert operations. Among the former were Manuel Antonio "Tony" de Varona, Miguel Suárez Fernández and the brothers José and Eduardo Suárez Rivas.

2) A second (opposition) group from within the Auténtico Party, headed by Dr. Grau San Martín, aspiring to regain power. Grau had been encouraged to form this new party, which weakened the Auténtico Party block. In July 1951, Senator Santiaguito Rey Pernas became Grau's confidant, inspiring contradictions and ambitions among supporters of Grau and Prío.

3) A third force, represented by the Ortodoxo Party (following the death of Chibás) which would win the elections of 1952. This party was also full of contradictions, because, in many places in the country, it was already in the hands of traditional politicians and landowners.[1]

4) The old Marxist party and once-powerful Cuban labor movement; harassed, persecuted and repressed. According to U.S. analysts, the

Cuban revolutionary left was in no condition to organize resistance to any new political offensive by the right wing, including a coup d'état.

5) The Batista group, with its old political-military leadership. Batista had been repudiated by the whole population, and seemed to have no possibility of returning to power in Cuba.

U.S. dominance of Cuba was absolute by 1950-52 and the craftsmen of the coup d'état of March 10, 1952, belonged to the same forces that had fashioned the imperialist domination: the alliance of U.S. financial-Mafia-intelligence groups.

The intelligence-Mafia alliance was in charge of covert operations, using elements of the political-military leadership of the traditional parties. Secret structures of the country's armed institutions were also subordinated to special agencies of the United States.

A picture (albeit partial) can now begin to be assembled of the great conspiracy. By way of historical background, it must be pointed out that at the beginning of the protectorate period (1902), the United States organized intelligence services within the constitutional army in Cuba. In addition, U.S. espionage — both within and outside the island — was conducted against the independence movements.

The United States came to directly control the intelligence agencies of the armed forces after the first military intervention, with the advent of the pseudo republic. Some U.S. intelligence specialists even assumed Cuban citizenship.

They trained agents, not just on the island but in the United States itself. In general, these agents were recruited when they began their studies in the military academies. They were present as well in the operations that made it possible for Machado to abandon the country in the 1930s. They also participated in maneuvers that made Batista the most important figure through whom the United States imposed its rule over Cuba.

In keeping with the changing times, they considerably widened their spectrum — with politicians, lawyers, journalists, gangsters, businessmen, *mafiosi* and senior executives all playing a part. Consequently, no one on the island could make a political or military move of any significance without the U.S. intelligence services knowing the background to events from the beginning. It is necessary to point out that the U.S. intelligence-Mafia alliance that prepared for the coup d'état of March 10, 1952, was more powerful than the groups that intervened in September 1933. Twenty years had passed (including another world war), and the intelligence community had reached greater supremacy in U.S. foreign affairs.

The great surge began in 1940, when President Roosevelt sent William J. Donovan (a New York lawyer) to travel to England and areas of the Mediterranean and Balkans, with the intention of gathering and evaluating information. Donovan returned with the mission fulfilled and this recommendation: the United States should establish a central intelligence organization.

From his proposal came the Office of Coordination of Information, on June 13, 1942. Donovan himself directed the office and that same year there began a strategic alliance between the U.S. intelligence services and the U.S. Mafia.

The office was divided into two big operative centers: the Office of Strategic Services (OSS), under the charge of Donovan; and the Office of War Information. The OSS became famous for its military operations in Europe, Asia and southern Italy, and for employing the support of the secret structures of the Mafia, with "a pattern of combining special operations with information gathering that is still followed by the CIA."[2]

Since 1944, Donovan had prepared the plan for establishing a central intelligence agency. When Truman assumed power, he proceeded to close the OSS. Some of its agents went into army intelligence; others were transferred to the State Department, where they formed the Bureau of Intelligence and Investigation.

Four months later on January 22, 1946, an executive order created the National Intelligence Authority, and a Central Intelligence Group, precursor of the CIA. On May 1, 1947, (two or three weeks after Lucky Luciano left Cuba), Truman named Rear Admiral Roscoe H. Hillenkoetter as the man in charge. Roscoe spoke three languages and had several years' experience in naval intelligence, the organization that began contacts with the U.S. Mafia. According to the investigator

Penny Lernoux, Lucky Luciano was a "famous *mafioso* who set up the Asian network for the import of heroin into the United States; and a key figure in the OSS/CIA alliance with the underworld."[3]

It must also be pointed out that another key figure in forging these alliances was Meyer Lansky. As Frederic Sondern Jr. wrote:

> Most detail of what happened from here on is still classified information in Pentagon files. An angry Senator Estes Kefauver, with all the authority of a congressional investigating committee behind him, tried to get at the facts in 1951. He had little success. The navy, members of District Attorney Hogan's office and everybody else who really knew anything were and remain vague for a good reason.[4]

The National Security Act that authorized the creation of the CIA in 1947, also established a Defense Department. It united the armed forces of the United States and created the National Security Council. The duties of the CIA were summarized in five brief paragraphs, granting the agency unlimited powers which, in fact, authorized it to pursue any action or alliance, even with organized crime, in the United States or in any other part of the world. Let us examine the third paragraph: "To correlate and evaluate intelligence relating to the national security, and provide for the appropriate dissemination of such intelligence within the government... Provided that the agency shall have no police, subpoena, law-enforcement powers, or internal-security functions."[5]

The CIA immediately began to be the coordinating element of the powerful U.S. intelligence community, made up of the National Security Council, Army Intelligence, Air Force Intelligence, the State Department Bureau of Intelligence and Research, the Atomic Energy Commission and the FBI. In addition, there were the CIA's own operative groups, in charge of special operations; plus the Pentagon's intelligence service, the Treasury Department's Narcotics Division, the Immigration and Naturalization Service and the secret agency of the U.S. Customs Office.

In the words of Allen W. Dulles: "The National Security Act of 1947... has given intelligence a more influential position in our government than intelligence enjoys in any other government of the world."[6]

By 1952, when the United States secretly initiated the coup d'état of March 10, they had an intelligence mechanism with which they were carrying out operations in various parts of the world. But in the case of the coup that installed Batista into power, the clandestine apparatus of the Mafia was also unleashed against Cuba, as were the investigative and information services of the financial groups established in Havana. Elements of the political-military leadership of the traditional parties were also involved. So too was Cuba's police apparatus, which had always been subordinated to the U.S. intelligence services.

The motives for the coup d'état of March 10, 1952, resulted from a combination of factors, both internal and external. In order to undertake the coup d'état of March 1952, U.S. imperialism took advantage of the chaos that was sweeping across the country, caused by the Auténtico Party. Corruption was boundless. A ferocious McCarthyism persecuted the revolutionary left and repressed the Cuban labor movement. Gangsterism prevailed. The Prío brothers perpetuated economic, moral and political disorder. But in spite of it all, the resistance of the Cuban people was growing stronger.

The demands of the vast majority developed into the vigorous moral campaign headed by Eduardo R. Chibás. This seriously threatened the interests of the United States, which had established the criminal state within Cuba. Popular rebellion extended day by day, threatening to explode at any moment.

There was also the profound political, moral (and legal) crisis that overtook U.S. society between 1950-52. The crisis began when investigations of the Kefauver Commission revealed the existence of an extraordinary criminal world, which had great power, handled great fortunes and extended into all spheres of U.S. society. The threat represented by the revelations of the Kefauver Commission was directed not only at the Mafia's interests, but also at important sectors of the U.S. economy, its political structures and the increasingly powerful and active intelligence community in the United States.

The most immediate threat following the Kefauver Commission's revelations was to illegal businesses in the United States (had action against organized crime been prosecuted with any vigor).

Consequently, the American Mob began immediately to retreat to its prized exterior base. Cuba, by 1950, was the most important possession of U.S. organized crime outside the United States. It was logical that, given the situation that presented itself, the Mafia might try to reorganize its interests to make them more solid, stable and capable of resisting any external pressure, with governmental measures that made its business deals legal, or at least more tolerable.

These two factors — pressure to which the U.S. Mafia was being submitted within the United States itself, and moral campaigning on the part of Eduardo R. Chibás — accelerated preparations for the coup d'état, providing the vehicle through which General Batista resumed control of the country.

Batista presented the most reliable of possible options. He had demonstrated extraordinary loyalty toward the dominant financial groups, the Mafia families and intelligence services of the United States. He was the most disciplined leader available, in a time when the very existence of the empire of Havana was being decided.

Nevertheless, it was exceedingly tricky for Washington to justify covert operations to reinstall General Batista to power, just as serious allegations were being made in the United States against criminal groups, and their influence in political, judicial sectors and economic spheres.

In a little less than 20 years, the alliance of the financial-Mafia-intelligence services had become close-knit in their interactions. For the coup d'état to be successful, it was necessary to achieve consensus among all the dominant forces. This fact might also partly explain the pretensions of the Prío brothers when, in 1950-51, they made an unusual bid to take part in the deals of U.S. companies about to open nickel mines in the east of Cuba. (The companies taking part were the American Smelting and Refining Company and the Freeport Sulfur Company, tied to the Rockefeller financial group, Guggenheim interests and the National City Bank.) The Prío brothers briefly snatched the Cuban nickel business away from the Rockefeller aligned financial interests and gave it to the Dutch Billiton company. They mounted a second challenge by declaring unlimited sugar production for 1951, when the U.S. Government was applying pressure to impose a policy of restriction on production, directed at improving the prices of raw sugar and stabilizing the international market at the expense of Cuban interests.

The Prío brothers' pretensions created a climate of extreme tension between the Auténtico Party government and the powerful Rockefeller clan, a decisive factor in Washington's authorization of the coup d'état of March 10.

By 1950, the mines of Cuba's Oriente Province were highly prized as sources of indispensable strategic material for the U.S. war industry. The Rockefeller-aligned financial complex, in turn, controlled important sugar and livestock businesses in Cuba: some 20 of the larger sugar mills, a little more than 1.326 million acres (40,000 *caballerías*) of land, plus the Becerra livestock company (better known as the King Ranch).

The Dulles brothers had substantial ties to companies interested in Cuban nickel, and to other important businesses in the eastern provinces, providing yet another reason for the events of 1952. Before they dedicated themselves to espionage activities,[7] Foster and Allen Dulles had maintained interests in businesses connected with the Wall Street law firm of Sullivan and Cromwell.

In 1952, John Foster Dulles was the U.S. Secretary of State; and his brother Allen Dulles was sub-director of the CIA, an agency he would soon direct until the early 1960s. Today, it can be affirmed that the Dulles brothers exercised a decisive role in the arrangements for Washington's authorization of the coup d'état, taking advantage of several situations that provided them with the pretext for their covert operations.

Seen in their historical context, the Prío brothers' plans seem unusually ambitious. They attempted to compete with massive financial groups, to challenge them and participate in spheres reserved exclusively for the great U.S. interests.

Carlos Prío was probably incited by some group or interest promising support for this project. In reality, however, Prío was giving the Dulles brothers powerful arguments for mounting a coup.

Yet the Dulles brothers could never be described as "ingenuous." Could these astute men really have been persuaded to believe that aggressive measures carried out against U.S. financial interests, by a government like that of the Auténtico Party, were due solely to a decision taken by the Cuban president? It was in fact a matter of "interrupting the farce of the representative democracy, which until now had been very useful, and promoting nothing less than a coup d'état."[8]

It was certainly very difficult (almost impossible) for Washington to argue in favor of a coup in Cuba, at a time when political scandals in the United States threatened the stability of the American Mob.

The Dulles brothers, however, were too experienced to overlook what was at stake, or to not notice the increasing integration of politics, the economy and organized crime in the United States.

U.S. intelligence activities in Cuba had never been so intense. There had never been so many operations to protect imperialist control in Cuba. For present generations to fully understand how Batista was able to return to Cuba, we must reflect upon the concept of the military coup d'état. The coup — just like all the other political changes of 1934-58 (when the criminal state was being formed) — was without a doubt the fruit of political arrangements. March 10 reflected the essential tone of this period of politics, which saw the widening and consolidation of the power of the United States "in attempts to bolster or undermine foreign governments."[9]

Some factors began to take shape from the very beginning of the political thrust of the Auténtico Party in 1944. Other factors have older historical origins. The remaining factors were a product of covert operations pursued by the U.S. intelligence community, using elements of the Auténtico-Batista leadership; or of clandestine activities carried out under the auspices of the U.S. Mafia, whose empire was seriously threatened.

An important factor was the repression of the old Marxist party and Cuban labor unions, by means of Chicago-style gangster tactics, which in a few years led to the Cuban labor movement's division and domination by criminal elements.

Another element was the historical absence of a true Cuban middle class. This economic class had emerged, during the 20th century, in a very precarious state, because of 30 years of anticolonial wars that had devastated the country. Members of this class found themselves living under U.S. occupation, and were immediately suppressed, while the imperialists began appropriating land, mines, transportation, communications, finance and, of course, the coveted sugar industry. Beaten by the crises of 1920 and 1929, this severely weakened sector of the Cuban economy also fell victim to the emergence of new financial groups in the 1930s.

In Cuba by 1950 there were economic sectors dependent on the financial interests of the United States and U.S. Mafia. The Cuban sectors were marginally related to other groups revolving around large landowners in agricultural or livestock businesses and real estate. Other elements appeared to be Cuban (Barletta, Battisti, Julio Lobo, etc.) when in reality they were foreigners or answered to foreign interests. There was a third group, consisting of "visible heads" of large concerns — senior executives, or people who spent a lot of money and boasted that they represented big businesses. There was also the political-military leadership of the government, whose fraudulent schemes allowed 20 new millionaires to step forth every four years.

Consequently, by 1950-52, the conscience of the nation, and any genuine concept of nationality, was maintained only in the revolutionary movement and by the vast popular masses. The pseudo-bourgeoisie groups and their dependents were incapable of resisting the installation of a military dictatorship promoted by Washington.

President Truman's foreign policy was favorable toward a coup d'état. It was characterized by great material aid to Western Europe (via the Marshall Plan) and indifference toward the grave economic and social problems of Latin America. This indifference was especially evident with regard to Central America, the countries of the Andes, Paraguay and long-suffering Haiti, for whose age-old misery the United States is directly responsible.

In Cuba, very important changes were taking place, which were surely noticed by the powerful U.S. intelligence community in Havana. In universities and other places political restlessness abounded, and there were exchanges of ideas and discussions among young people of various political tendencies. Some were of Ortodoxo politics, some from the Marxist left, and some represented the revolutionary thought of José Martí.

And so, the U.S. intelligence community proceeded to mount a series of operations to prevent the Cuban people from presenting organized resistance to the political-military leadership that would assume power with Batista. To achieve this, operations were aimed at:

1) Worsening the already intense climate of violence, to persuade important sectors that only an iron fist (Batista's) could return the nation to tranquility.

2) Cementing a greater bond between the leadership of the Auténtico and Batista parties and between important people who would become directly involved with reordering the criminal state. Auténtico Party figures such as Rolando Masferrer, Eusebio Mujal Barniol and Miguel Suárez Fernández, among others, would assume power immediately through dictatorship. Other persons such as Eduardo Suárez Rivas and Santiaguito Rey Pernas, to cite two examples, went on to legitimate positions, after having fulfilled missions close to the Auténtico Party.

3) The creation of a psychological climate so the entrance of military personnel into politics might be seen as the only solution to the grave problems confronting Cuba.

4) The application of a policy of dispersing the oppositional forces. This political strategy had been applied since the first military intervention; and, during the 1930s, it constituted the essential objective of imperialism, which was to prevent genuine unity among the revolutionary forces in Cuba.

5) The Mafia (by means of front companies) under the charge of the Barletta family, along with Ángel Cambó and the firm of Humara y Lastra, among others, came to control important communications media, such as the newspaper *El Mundo,* the national Unión Radio y Televisión, Channel 2 and other media.

6) The reinforcement of the police apparatus: 250 new officers, on permanent patrol throughout Greater Havana. The prominent figure would be Lieutenant Salas Cañizares [chief of police after the events of March 10] who commanded all those forces.

7) The signing of a military pact [48 hours before the coup d'état] between the Auténtico Party government and the United States. This maneuver made it possible for Batista to inherit an agreement that benefited him, and the prestige of Prío's government's was tarnished even further.[10]

The Auténtico Party leadership could have resisted the coup d'état. They had access to arms to confront the usurpers. If a truck full of firearms had been sent to the University of Havana or to some working class quarters of Havana, an interminable struggle would have begun.

Irrefutable evidence exists that the Auténtico Party leadership knew about preparations for the military agreement. According to his own confession, Prío's vice-president, Guillermo Alonso Pujol, had been meeting secretly with Dr. Jorge García Montes and General Batista regarding the coup d'état since March 1951:

> The next day, very early, I was in Kuquine. My host, to the extent he thought appropriate, revealed the secret to me. "In the army," he began to say, "there is a movement of young officers working toward the destitution of President Prío, and toward his substitution by the vice-president of the republic. They see me as the figure who should give the movement a historic tone. If we do not listen to them, we run the risk that they will do it on their own and this is very dangerous given the military's absence of a sense of political orientation." Although he did not say it clearly, he spoke to me as though there were a coup about to be executed in the hours immediately following.[11]

Prío's own intelligence services were aware of the military plot and they had been repeatedly informed of the movements and meetings that were taking place. In a report of the SIM [Military Intelligence Service] taken from SIM File No. 33, of 1952, essential aspects of the conspiracy have been established:

> FIRST: That for approximately a year, the officer informant, with agents under his orders, has been maintaining a constant and discreet vigilance over the activities of ex-President Batista, in fulfillment of superior orders and because of having had news that he was maintaining political relations with members of the army on active service.
>
> SECOND: That in the course of these actions, it has been confirmed that ex-President Batista is surrounded by a plentiful group of retired military men who, for their part, attempt by all means to maintain contact with the troops on active service, preventing the need for the army to stage a coup d'état in favor of Batista, according to what he has said in intimate conversations.

THIRD: That last Saturday, January 26, in the offices of the PAU, located at No. 306, 17th Street, in Vedado, ex-President Batista met with a group of the aforementioned retired military men… In the said meeting they addressed the difficulty of the political panorama for Batista's presidential aspirations… They discussed the necessity of arriving at power violently with the support of the army…

FOURTH: Upon the conclusion of the meeting, Batista convoked his propaganda directors to a meeting that took place that very night at Finca Kuquine, during which plans were drawn up to modify the propaganda on the radio and in the press with the objective of… 1) Creating a climate of national concern intended to demonstrate that the current government lacks the strength to control order, to maintain public peace, and to guarantee property rights and free enterprise. 2) To influence public opinion that only Batista can reestablish this equilibrium, which has been interrupted…

FIFTH: That last night, February 7, a new meeting between the retired military personnel and ex-President Batista took place at Finca Kuquine, during which they considered the difficulty of the political situation… They came to an agreement in this meeting to accelerate the contacts with military personnel on active service with the objective of using them if a coup d'état were deemed necessary…

SIXTH: That those first meetings held in the month of January by Batista and the retired military men, and later by his directors of propaganda, were known to Kuchilán and gave origin to the note that appeared in a section of *Prensa Libre* on January 30 of the current year.[12]

There has been much speculation about Carlos Prío's reaction to the coup d'état; but like the advent of the Auténtico Party in 1944, the events of March 10 were the outcome of pressures applied and arrangements made among various factions. More than a military agreement, this careful job of "pressures and arrangements" was carried out, accompanied by much deception, with the direct intervention of U.S. imperialism.

A group of important people close to President Prío, and within the Auténtico Party leadership, knew about this objective, and collaborated to achieve it. They were present for the deals and compromises. They included, to mention just a few: Guillermo Alonso Pujol (vice-president of the republic); Rolando Masferrer (congressman, newspaper director and chief of one of the largest gangster groups); and Eusebio Mujal Barniol (who had usurped the leadership of the Cuban labor movement). The group included Senator Miguel Suárez Fernández (greatly influential in the Auténtico Party senatorial majority). There was also Eduardo Suárez Rivas. Immediately, or soon after, almost all of them crossed over to the group of politicians ruled by Batista — except for those who had to fulfill more delicate missions.

In August 1951, a psychological campaign was carried out against the Prío brothers. As part of systematic harassment, Pujol began to threaten the interests of the presidential family. In the last months of their government, the Prío family found itself in a desperate situation. If the Ortodoxo Party was to assume power, the people would demand the moral program of Eduardo R. Chibás become a reality.[13] If that happened, of course, important interests would be threatened.

Threats against the Prío family were designed to make the coup d'état acceptable, to make it appear that politics in Cuba were out of control and required a drastic intervention. It also helped to create a façade, as though the coup had emerged purely out of local political conditions.

Although the Prío family possessed millions of dollars in foreign banks, they were making strong investments within the country and buying estates and sugar refineries with money stolen from the state. The fact that they had invested tens of millions of dollars in Cuba made them vulnerable, susceptible to threats and blackmail.

In declarations to the press (such as Gastón Baquero's interview with Santiaguito Rey Pernas) the campaign to threaten the Prío family was stimulated even further. At the same time, public opinion was being manipulated so the masses demanded action be taken against the family.

The intelligence services and Mafia, attempting to create a perception that would make Batista appear as the only option, manufactured a climate of terror around the Prío family. In the final months, the Prío family was practically paralyzed. Rumors were increasing that as soon as the Ortodoxo Party took power family

The Mafia financier, Meyer Lansky.

Charles "Lucky" Luciano

"Lucky" Luciano at the Havana race track.

Umberto Anastasio (Albert Anastasia) and his lawyer.

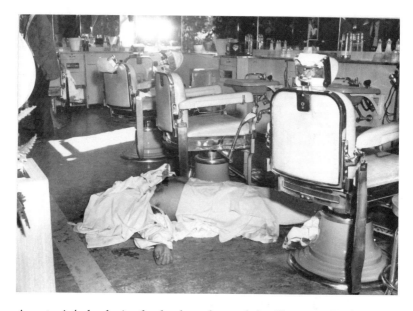

Anastasio's body in the barber shop of the Sheraton Park Hotel where he was assassinated.

Amadeo Barletta Barletta

Amleto Battisti

Don Vito Genovese

Santo Trafficante Jr.

U.S. Ambassador Smith presents his credentials in Havana, July 1957.

Batista and Sumner Welles (U.S. Ambassador to Cuba) at a reception at the Cuban Embassy in Washington.

Ramón Grau San Martín

U.S. actor George Raft, who managed the Hotel Capri on behalf of the Mafia.

Ava Gardner and her husband, Frank Sinatra, on a visit to Cuba.

Aerial view of the Hotel Nacional de Cuba, frequented by many of the Havana *mafiosi*.

Exterior, Tropicana nightclub.

At the Montmartre Casino.

The Tropicana nightclub in 1953.

Roulette in one
of the casinos of
Havana.

Gaspar Pumarejo and
his famous TV program,
"Queen for a Day."

Fulgencio Batista at West Point Military Academy, USA.

The Havana branch of the National City Bank of New York,
the most important foreign bank operating in Cuba.

General Fulgencio Batista and U.S. President Franklin D. Roosevelt in Washington. Batista was guest of honor at the White House in 1942.

members would be arrested, indicted and shot in La Cabaña and their property seized.

Each day that passed, it became clearer to the Prío family — Antonio and Paco had been meeting secretly with Batista in Miami — that Batista's return to power was a kind of salvation (the only salvation). He was the iron hand that would save them from popular wrath.

Experienced troops were used to carry out the coup of 1952. In addition, senior CIA officers took operational control of vital positions:

> Days before the coup d'état, Elliot Roosevelt (son of Franklin D. Roosevelt) arrived in Cuba interested in buying the second largest radio station in the country (RHC) and in establishing several businesses of various proportions. It is known that he had several private meetings with Batista. On Monday, March 10, after the coup had been carried out, Elliot Roosevelt communicated by telephone with Washington from the Hotel Nacional and informed an unidentified person that everything had gone according to plan. The day that Batista was installed in the palace as "chief of state," he was visited by Roosevelt, accompanied by powerful U.S. shipping magnates who, according to reports in the press, "limited themselves to a greeting." A U.S. officer was in Columbia, the military camp that was the center of the conspiracy and of the coup d'état, from the beginning of the events until the Prío Government fell. Two officers of the Caimanera naval base were in the army barracks of Santiago de Cuba on March 10, from dawn up until when the coup had been carried out and the military commands had been changed.[14]

U.S. intelligence was also preparing the ideological terrain in the United States. On September 5, 1951, Edward Tomlinson, spokesman for powerful U.S. interests, published an article in a chain of U.S. newspapers. Tomlinson offered an analysis of the situation in Cuba, pointing out that it had become quite complicated since the death of Chibás; and that Prío's labor union leaders (Eusebio Mujal Barniol, among others) were preparing to overthrow Prío. Tomlinson added that Batista was winning growing prestige thanks to the support of the army. Consequently, sensible Cubans thought that the best thing that could happen was that a coup d'état might occur to place a person of strong character in the government.[15] The analysis reveals: 1) that the details of the coup were carefully outlined; 2) that this project had been taking shape since August 1950; 3) that from the beginning it was aimed at reinstalling General Batista into power.[16]

It can be inferred that Batista did not have operational control of the coup of March 10 until it was quite advanced. That is, until he was already in military command of the camp at Columbia and central command of the army, navy and police services had been taken. Evidently, there were two operations. One was more visible and preparations for it consisted of meetings and persuasion of key people in military groups. The other was covert, under the charge of the intelligence services, acting for U.S. intelligence in Havana, which directed operations.

The coup of March 10 took place without mishap or immediate resistance from the Cuban people. Only three or four military personnel were killed in the vicinity of the presidential palace, because of a skirmish or misunderstanding. The Prío brothers retreated into exile — in a few hours they were out of the country. The Prío family left Cuba offended and outraged, because a group of military personnel had stripped them of the legitimate power granted to them in a constitutional manner by the people.

Yet at first, the Prío family was the greatest beneficiary of the military coup — economically, politically and in terms of perceived morality. The new regime, as was to be expected, never legally questioned the thefts, misdeeds, and systematic robberies of the humiliated president, which amounted to hundreds of millions of pesos.

Of course, Prío and his political-military leadership immediately switched over to the opposition (without giving up their ties with U.S. intelligence services and the U.S. Mafia). His group presented themselves as a new option, aspiring to return to power, trying to maintain this façade even during the insurrection of the revolutionary forces led by Fidel Castro.

Money Laundering and Front Companies

On December 22, 1950, Dr. Felipe Pazos, president of the Banco Nacional de Cuba [BNC], granted Amadeo Barletta Barletta License No. 62 to convert the Banco Internacional de La Habana into the Banco Atlántico.[1]

Thereafter, the Banco Atlántico had its offices on the ninth floor of the building at No. 16 Menocal Avenue, previously Infanta Avenue. Later it would be on the ground floor of the building on the corner of 23rd Street and P, on the street known as La Rampa in Vedado, the same building occupied by the distribution company for General Motors in Cuba, of which Barletta was a director.

The Banco Atlántico opened its operations with the following executives: president, Amadeo Barletta Barletta; vice-president, Amadeo H. Barletta Jr. (Barlettica); secretary, Dr. Luis J. Botifoll and general manager, Dr. Leonardo Masoni.

From its beginnings, functionaries of the BNC monitored the operations of the Banco Atlántico; but affairs in the delinquent state were arranged and manipulated in such a manner that the bank never confronted any problems. This was equally true during the administration of Dr. Carlos Prío Socarrás, and afterwards, when Batista's dictatorship was installed.

At the beginning, the Banco Atlántico denied it had any ties with affiliated or subsidiary companies. What is more, on May 29, 1951,

Dr. Leonardo Masoni, in a letter sent to the BNC, pointed out that his bank had no ties of this kind whatsoever. A few weeks later, on July 30, 1951, Amadeo Barletta Barletta himself sent a letter to the BNC, assuring the latter that the Banco Atlántico had no relations with affiliated societies or companies.[2]

On August 7, 1951, however, the chief of bank inspection of the BNC (Miguel Termes) discovered the existence of a numerous group of subsidiary companies (fronts for the Mafia) and, in his report to Dr. Felipe Pazos, Termes explained:

> On dates prior to the inspection, the bank reported in its monthly balance sheets the absence of affiliated companies or of some affiliated holding company.
>
> Upon carrying out the inspection of this entity in August 1951, it was determined that the company Santo Domingo Motor Corporation, constituted under the laws of the Dominican Republic, represented in reality an affiliated holding company, possessor of more than 50 percent of the stock of the Banco Atlántico. Credentials in the name of this company were not shown to the inspectors.
>
> Furthermore, relationships with 18 other companies were established. They were: Caribbean Sales Association, Constructora Andes S.A., Compañía Editorial El Mundo (written press, including a newspaper and other publications),[3] La Flor de Tibes (coffee), Victor G. Mendoza, Compañía Inversiones Gilispa, Compañía General de Comercio e Industria, Compañía Inmobilaria Motor Center, Compañía Inmobilaria Betis, Compañía de Inversiones Bacaro, Importadora Cinzano de Cuba, La Filosofía (department store), La Unión y el Fénix de Cuba Compañía Nacional de Seguros, Ambar Motors Corporation, Servicios Radio Móvil, Rabna Auto Corporation, Compañía Fiduciaria Inversionista and Compañía Financiera Inversionista Panamericana.[4]

In the conclusion to his report to the BNC, Mr. Termes pointed out the vertiginous "pyramid structure of the business affairs of the Banco Atlántico."

Responding on August 31, 1951, Amadeo Barletta Barletta communicated to the BNC that the demands of the bank inspection group were not fulfilled in due time "because of an error of interpretation which we lament,"[5] assuring that he had given instructions to the functionaries of the Banco Atlántico "so that they may proceed to eliminate as soon as possible the problems indicated by the inspection."[6]

But the Mafia was not disposed to fulfilling any promise. It had no reason to do so. The Banco Atlántico continued its tactics of misinformation. Errors were tolerated, mistakes pardoned and problems of interpretation ignored. There were also many "involuntary" slips of memory, which the manager Masoni could always excuse with a simple letter to the BNC, generally requesting that the difficulties be overlooked.[7] The Barletta family's bank never faced any problem, not from its founding in 1949, in the period in which the BNC was directed by Felipe Pazos; nor after the coup d'état of 1952, when Dr. Joaquín Martínez Sáenz held the directorship.

In a very cunning manner (as if it were aware that things were arranged from above), the Inspection Department of the BNC informed Dr. Joaquín Martínez Sáenz, in 1953, of the following:

> The administration [of the Banco Atlántico] is deemed efficient, but not secure, if one considers that the institution's credit policy is in the exclusive power of its president, Mr. A. Barletta, and its general director, Dr. L. Masoni, who pay more attention to their personal knowledge of their debtors than they do to an analysis of their economic and financial status.[8]

The Banco Atlántico maintained a great façade of proper management, legitimacy and scrutiny. In reality, however, it enjoyed all kinds of privileges and special allowances. It had no reason to worry about a simple report affecting its impunity.

A characteristic of the Banco Atlántico was its apparent carelessness in financial affairs, reflected in the reports it periodically issued. In spite of the fact that the BNC knew of constant violations in its trading and operations with U.S. currency, one method of erasing any trace of this was the use of inadequate registers, in which returned checks were supposed to be recorded. Notes were made on loose sheets, which were often thrown away or lost. The bank's reports reflected constant omissions. In addition, the operations were not recorded in the registries, nor were the checks or sums deposited. The bank did not even keep records of withdrawals and deposits.[9]

Documents dated March 10, 1953,[10] reveal that the inspectors of the BNC began to report repeated violations in the direct cashing of checks, drawn by front companies from the 23rd Street branch of the National City Bank of New York. These were checks without control, issued in Cuban currency and paid at the tellers' windows of the bank in U.S. currency, without these operations being legalized.

Another maneuver of the Banco Atlántico that aroused much attention was an item of credit granted to the Belmoy Trading Company for purchases in Germany, without proper control.[11] On March 11, 1953, a report from the bank inspectors observed that the Banco Atlántico lacked an auditor and that there were frequent violations of statutes. The report underscored the fact that, although the bank was quite solvent, it applied an unhealthy credit policy, because it lacked information about credits and balances. For this reason, the inspectors reached the conclusion that this information was concealed, to avoid giving information about the bank's relations and business affairs.[12]

The new chief of the group of bank inspectors, Sergio Valdés Rodríguez, in a report to Dr. Joaquín Martínez Sáenz, characterized the Banco Atlántico and its directorship as persons given to bold business practices. He said, "as in many other banks inspected, there is an almost total lack of information about credits and balances, and we suspect that the bank is hiding this information."[13]

In this period, hundreds of millions of dollars from the United States were passing through Havana. Numerous fortunes needed to be legalized. For these arrangements to be carried out, apart from the banks being required to facilitate them, it was necessary to use a great number of front companies and businesses that were capable of recirculating immense capital.

In the first days of January 1953, BNC inspectors had already detected typical "laundering" operations: Ambar Motors Corporation had drawn Check No. 6551 on November 5, 1952, to the order of Ambar Motors, on Account No. 1570, in the name of M. R. Leeder.

Valdés Rodríguez, chief inspector of the BNC, in a confidential letter to the Banco Agrícola y Mercantil, informed the latter that it had paid substantial sums in the name of the Banco Atlántico. He then requested that the Banco Agrícola y Mercantil:

> ...investigate to see if those checks were paid in cash, given that the vouchers for these checks specify that they have been paid in cash. Confidentially, we inform you that we have news that these checks have been paid in U.S. money, for which reason we would appreciate your investigating the matter thoroughly, because we do not see what benefit the Banco Agrícola y Mercantil obtained by paying them, especially considering that they were for substantial quantities — almost half a million dollars — and considering as well that they were in the name of another bank.[14]

In January, 1953, other fraudulent operations of the Banco Atlántico were discovered. Ambar Motors Corporation and the Caribbean Sales Association had drawn, in December 1952, a group of checks for the value of a million pesos in Cuban currency against the Banco Atlántico. But these checks were not cashed in the bank of Amadeo Barletta Barletta, but taken to the principal offices of the National City Bank of New York, on O'Reilly and Compostela Streets, and cashed at a teller's window in U.S. currency. Consequently, the BNC inspection group, which had seriously questioned these operations, denounced them on January 23, 1953. In a letter directed to the bank, Sergio Valdés wrote: "Regarding the currency, we are interested in knowing if the payment has been made in U.S. money, something that you can verify easily through the records of the cashier or of the reserve from the date that the payments were effected."[15]

Given that the operation was unscrupulous, the bank's reply was frankly ingenuous:

> In answer to your letter of the 8th day of the current month [B. Fulgenzi, general manager of the National City Bank of New York in Havana, wrote to Sergio Valdés, chief of Bank Inspection of the BNC] in reference to various checks paid to Ambar Motors Corporation, and to the Caribbean Sales Association, Inc., we wish to make manifest to you that said checks were paid to the very firms mentioned, according to the endorsements

that appear on the same. Given that important quantities are in question, we thought it appropriate to cash these checks directly at the Banco Atlántico without feeling that we were violating the regulations of the Chamber of Compensation.

As for the currency in which the payments were made, we are sorry that we cannot establish that information because we have no record of that detail. On some occasions the cashiers note this detail on the back of the checks themselves for their convenience in case they have a discrepancy, but as the checks are not in our hands, it is impossible for me in this case to determine if they were handled this way.[16]

What is certain is that these checks were cashed at a teller's window in U.S. money without any type of control or verification, which is especially odd given the fact that the checks were for such large sums. No record was made in registers or books, so the operation left no trace. An hour after the checks had been cashed, the cashier of the National City Bank had already appeared personally in the offices of the Banco Atlántico to cash the checks in Cuban currency without the checks' passing through the Chamber of Compensation.

The affiliated or front companies of the Barletta family had the same executives. The presidents, vice-presidents, secretaries and treasurers were always Giovanni Spada, Amadeo Barletta Barletta, Amadeo H. Barletta Jr., José Manuel Martínez Zaldo, José Guash Prieto, Francisco de Paudo, Próspero Zauchi, Ramiro Ortiz y de la Vega and other famous names.

The Barletta family possessed substantial interests in pharmaceutical laboratories. Through investments or loans, they had also come to dominate the Compañía Tropical de Motores and the Compañía de Transporte Ómnibus La Ranchuelera. The credit policy of the U.S. Mafia placed within their reach companies such as the Compañía de Ómnibus Santiago-Habana and the Terminal de Ómnibus, with Francisco Vidal and Enrique Caucedo[17] carrying out the necessary operations.

The Barletta group conducted substantial operations with numerous limited liability companies, including Fernando Munilla Soliño, Zaldo Martínez, Productos Químicos Robes, Publicidad Méndez, Eugenio Riverol, Goodyear de Cuba, Ross y Hermano and many others.[18]

The Banco Atlántico also engaged in important business affairs with diverse limited liability institutions and companies, such as the Compañía Inmobilaria Alma, Editorial Ellas, Minerva Industrial and Nueva Compañía Azucarera Gómez Mena, to name a few.[19] This new method of manipulating finances, of course, facilitated the dominance of various companies.

Since his rise to power (and in response to the commitments he had made), Batista devoted himself to the task of creating a group of institutions of extraordinary reach, to help realize the plans of the U.S. Mafia in Cuba. In view of the new and promising prospects, the Mafia families installed in Havana also began a process of reorganization. On March 1, 1954, the Banco Atlántico announced its liquidation. The measure, logically, was aimed at perfecting the operational capacity of its business affairs in order to use entities with recognized experience, prestige and professionalism. Greater efficiency was necessary, especially for matters in which no trace should be left. The solid banking entity, The Trust Company of Cuba, then surprised everybody by taking steps toward a merger with the Banco Atlántico. In a most remarkable manner, beginning on April 20, 1954, The Trust Company of Cuba assumed the interests of the Barletta family.

In those months, as Frederic Sondern Jr. would describe years later,[20] the premises were being created for a state that placed itself at the service of the U.S. Mafia. A new era was beginning, in which "political connections were formidable, reaching well into President Batista's palace."[21] Barletta's Mafia group, for its part, also began to effect operations at that time, through the Banco Financiero, using a "visible head" who came to dominate a great sugar-producing empire.

* * *

The empire of Havana functioned as a giant corporation, with multiple specialized departments, which differed greatly from the traditional structures of the Sicilian Mafia during its early establishment in the United States.

To mask or supplement its illicit operations, the Mafia increasingly employed the various legal means available to contemporary capitalism for the organization of it interests: laws, agreements, cover-ups, a veneer of respectability and so on. In the latter years, however, the Mafia families in Havana depended not only on the initial power they had established in Cuba since 1934. With the extension of their business affairs, and following conflicts with other U.S. criminal groups, they had also allowed for the entrance of new allies.

Just as the scheme of imperialist domination relied on multiple links being maintained between interest groups, the Mafia families maintained multiple connections — to further the organization, exploitation and control of their business affairs in Cuba.

The interests that the empire of Havana possessed could be grouped into the following "administrations":

1) The promotion of a grand, international (principally U.S.) tourist industry based on hotel-casinos, recreation centers, large and medium-sized cabarets and chains of nightclubs, all operated in an absolutely legal manner. Even the *mafiosi*, from El Cejudo "Bushy-Eyebrows" Lansky — brother of Meyer Lansky — to the brothers Joe and Charles Sileci, appeared on the Social Security rolls in Cuba. These business deals generated many other activities. An example: schools for card dealers or for specialists in various aspects of organized gambling. These schools not only trained professionals for Cuba but for other places in the Caribbean, Central and South America and the United States.

2) Channels for drug traffic: heroin for the United States and cocaine for consumption in Cuba. This extraordinarily lucrative branch had a compartmentalized structure. To allow for the consumption of drugs, especially cocaine (in the highest circles or in the Mafia's installations), the drug administration enjoyed an absolute tolerance.

3) Other modes of gambling and betting games, such as those played at the Havana race track, the Frontón Jai Alai (dog races every day) and forms that had a more popular character: boxing, numbers games, charades, bingo, slot machines, etc.

4) The appraisal and trade of precious gems.

5) Groups in charge of specialized prostitution. (One of the best known was Marina's chain of houses, which provided services to the luxury hotels.) In Havana, the Mafia also kept prostitutes destined

ond the crises of 1920 and 1929. And the country
ore dependent on imports after the formation of the

of the 1950s, Cuba's role as a mono-producer and
was an economic straightjacket that strangled the
nterests.

1925, one could observe a "progressive tendency
ction of sugar exportation and... sugar production."[3]
owever, the situation became increasingly unbearable,
protectionist tariffs and the implementation of the
or the exportation of Cuban sugar destined for the

al maneuvers carried out by sugar interests, acting
other economic and financial interests of the United
Cuba from shifting into other industries (or industrial
used on sugar derivatives). Collusion even made the
of agriculture impossible, and the development of a
e was likewise prevented.

statistics, Cuba participated in 50 percent of U.S.
ion before 1925, and this was reduced to 28.6 percent
ary to what has been sometimes asserted, World
strengthen the Cuban middle class or boost banking
ctors such that they could begin to rival U.S. banking.
nsistently overlooked the fact that, beginning in the
ame the largest financial center for the "laundering"
s originating in the United States, which constituted
economy in the country. Many schemes and interests
umbrella of this banking process. Some banks appear
s, forming part of the Clearing House of Havana, such
mpany of Cuba. Only later, in an almost magical act,
pany of Cuba became ruled by Cuban groups, who
o the most important bank in the country — more
the Chase Manhattan Bank or Citibank. In reality,
d activities of these so-called Cuban banks have not
ed.

for other areas of the Caribbean and the United States. This does not
include the many other women who resorted to prostitution because
of poverty, who in the 1950s numbered 100,000.

6) The organization of contraband, from sumptuous articles
(luxury cars, gold, electronic equipment, etc.) to diverse trinkets, all
of which passed through duty-free zones, ports and airports, airline
and maritime companies, etc. This contraband was also transported
through the military airport of Columbia.

7) The fostering and control (through their exploitation and/
or use) of legal businesses under the charge of import and export
companies: department stores, large distribution agencies, airline
companies, pharmaceutical laboratories and insurance companies.
Also, the use or control of banking networks, transportation
companies and sugar mills. All kinds of companies were operated
by this "administration."

8) Links with the international financial center located in Havana,
for the legalization of immense fortunes. The financial groups that
controlled the Cuban economy, in the traditional sense, received great
benefits. For the empire of Havana to stay well oiled, it was necessary
for each of the parties to receive its share of the spoils.

9) The occupation and control of important means of mass
communication, both within and outside Cuba; for marketing and
publicity purposes, public relations and international propaganda.

10) Those overseeing political relations between Cuba and the
United States. By the 1950s (the coronation of this period) the principal
task of this administration was to increasingly finance Batista as the
principal "visible head" of the apparent power in Cuba.

11) The administration in charge of intelligence and its collaborators;
this branch was also in charge of the armed branch of the Mafia families
of Havana.

12) A central or general administration for the control of the
empire. This included the headquarters of the U.S. Mafia in Cuba, its
operative centers and its structure of internal dominion.

It is impossible to present a comprehensive investigation of all the
Mafia's activities in Cuba, under all of the above categories. Instead, a
detailed historical examination of some of the great and famous hotel-

casinos and similar establishments is given in Appendix One. It is
an absorbing study, and shows the intricate connections between the
various interest groups and institutions that were involved, including
those operating from behind the scenes.

A similarly detailed examination of the creation of the Banco de La
Habana (later, Banco Financiero) and important changes to the Cuban
sugar industry is given in Appendix Two.

Trade and Econom

For a complete understandin
on Cuba beginning in 1934,
The work of Dr. Julio Le Riv
economic cycle had closed, bu
in the Cuban economy. It wa
for exportation in great quanti
Cuban nation had only two alte
to the United States, or it devot
of what it was importing."[2]

The great tragedy confronti
United States over the Cuban
mono-exporter, Cuba could n
market. It possessed nickel,
produced a certain amount of t
necessities, however, it depen
taking into account that as muc
consumed by Cubans was imp
even imported icecream, candy

The old Cuban economic struct
of colonialism, was greatly reinfo
from the first stages of the Cuban
to be a mono-producer and mor

the world) be
became much
criminal state.

By the star
mono-exporte
country's vital

Beginning
toward the rec
From 1934 on,
with a policy
quota metho
U.S. market.

Conspirat
in concert wi
States, imped
development
diversificatic
merchant m

Accordin
sugar consu
by 1932. Cc
War II did
and financia
People hav
1940s, Cuba
of illicit for
an undergr
came unde
as foreign e
as The Tru
The Trust
converted
important
the under
been fully

It is undeniable that Washington was manipulating the country's sugar production, as a means of controlling the Cuban economy. It is also true that, in the latter years, the United States was more interested in dominating the sugar industry through the manipulation of hundreds of millions of dollars in market-entry tariffs, which Cuban sugar had to pay to the United States.

Such was the straightjacket the United States imposed on Cuba, by means of the sugar industry, that the country could not even search for new markets. The quota mechanism demanded an extensive list of preferential tariffs, placed upon hundreds of industrial and agricultural products. The U.S. market rapidly displaced European producers from Cuba, gradually closing off the country's commercial and financial prospects.

By 1934, commerce to Cuba involved a preferential list of some "400 lines of specified U.S. products."[4] In the established agreements, Cuba could not alter the tariffs "without prior consultation and negotiation."[5] Export and import was subjected entirely to the United States, and substantial sectors of the Cuban economy were ruined: shoes, fabrics, dairy products, etc., which had reached something of a peak during the 1920s. This resulted in declining revenue per capita, while spawning "small groups with very, very high income, in contrast to the general mass of the impoverished population."[6]

By 1920-25, Cuban income per capita was a third (33 percent) of that of the United States.

In 1952, the per capita income was less than a fifth (18 percent) of that of the United States.

	1925	1953
Sugar exportation per capita (tons)	1.56	0.89
Value of sugar per capita	86.0	64.0

Beginning in 1934, the tendency toward large-scale land ownership was reinforced in Cuba. The sugar industry, in the 1950s, possessed almost six million acres (180,000 *caballerías*) of land, of which it used only about three million acres (90,000 *caballerías*). According to

Dr. Julio Le Riverend, "Cuba, progressively, headed toward an agrarian structure based totally on large land ownership."[7]

Statistics (in U.S. dollars) for U.S. investments reveal:

1920	(more than)	1 billion
1936		666 million
1950		657 million
1954		713 million

Between 1934 and 1956, U.S. investments in Cuba produced a profit of between US$650 million and US$700 million,[8] of which only US$150 million was reinvested.

Cuba's economic life was determined by the "mono-producing and mono-exporting structure of the national economy. Meanwhile, sugar production occupied a predominant position as the economy became underdeveloped and the economic structure became deformed by the penetration of imperialist capital."[9]

Such was the economic-political situation of Cuba that, by 1950, the U.S. Government sent a commission of 17 experts from the International Bank for Reconstruction and Development (the World Bank) to Havana, to undertake an analysis of the situation.

By then, even U.S. imperialism began to fear that the McCarthy-like politics imposed on the Cuban nation could collapse. In the report of the Truslow Commission, besides the problems related to the economy, issues of a political nature were emphasized:

> War prosperity has created new standards of living for many of Cuba's people. If its economy cannot maintain these — at least in some reasonable degree — in less prosperous times, it will be subject to great political strains.
>
> If leaders have neglected to prepare Cuba for this, they will be held to blame by the people. And, if that should happen, control may well pass into subversive but specious hands — as it has done in other countries whose leaders have ignored the trends of the times."[10]

Applying political analysis to the economic circumstances, the group of specialists from the World Bank recommended remedial measures:

To make Cuba less dependent on sugar by promoting additional activities — not by curtailing sugar production. To expand existing — and to create new — industries, producing sugar by-products or using sugar as a raw material... To vigorously promote non-sugar exports... To stimulate tourism, improve railroads, highways, waterworks, etc. Action by the government to improve the human resources of the nation through education, health measures, the dissemination of technical information, etc. To implement budgetary reforms and to achieve better administration of resources. [11]

The Truslow Commission submitted its conclusions in July 1951, when scandals prompted by the Kefauver Commission were at their height. It was also when a series of covert operations were being undertaken in Cuba, to manipulate the interests of the nation and to neutralize the growing rebelliousness of the Cuban population. Most importantly, however, the scheme proposed by the Truslow Commission was impossible to implement under the conditions imposed historically by U.S. imperialism.

Washington's foreign policy toward the island was to disregard the recommendations of the Truslow Commission, in spite of the grave deficiencies that this report presented. That document was used only to silence the people or to sustain their hopes, which historically were condemned to failure. A decade later (with the triumph of the Cuban Revolution) something similar occurred with the attempts to implement the Alliance for Progress in Latin America.

If the recommendations of the Truslow Report had been carried out, it would have signified a negation of U.S. economic policy toward Cuba. Imperialism would never have consented (and it never did consent) to the island's conversion into an economic power, not even one dominated by U.S. capital, because this would have created an internal market which, in its turn, would have fortified a national middle class, besides creating a powerful working class. The policy of the United States in Cuba, from its origins, was directed toward impeding any resistance to the economic, political and social order; toward making the Cuban pseudo-bourgeoisie increasingly weaker, ever more subservient, ever more incapable and corrupt. All this in spite of the fact that this class had already lost its chance of power, by proving unable to direct the popular anti-imperialist movement which, in search of social justice, overthrew Machado's dictatorship in August 1933.

It is interesting to observe how, in December 1951, Harry Truman, then president of the United States, while on a visit to Key West, made a declaration regarding Cuba. With the subtlety of omission, Truman pointed out the economic and political ties that the United States would maintain toward the island, ignoring the problems that had been raised in the conclusions of the Truslow Commission.

Furthermore, what Truman did and did not say (only three months before the coup d'état of March 10) constitutes a kind of message, one calming any doubts the dominant groups might have still harbored. Truman negated the recommendations of the Truslow Report. The course he encouraged was not one directed toward developing an agricultural-industrial economy, but rather a service economy. Within this service economy, which would take shape rapidly in Cuba, the groups that traditionally dominated the country would receive extremely privileged treatment in sectors that benefited increasingly from the spoils.

> I have always been [said Truman] quite well informed regarding the problems of Cuba. I know the vicissitudes and progress of that country which is our friend, which at all moments has demonstrated its affinity with the democratic projections of the United States...
>
> Someday, as soon as possible, I hope to have the opportunity to visit Cuba, where I know I will find the proverbial hospitality that has been witnessed by the thousands of U.S. tourists who visit that beautiful country annually.
>
> It is my sincerest desire that the welfare and the prosperity that Cuba currently enjoys continue in the future. I know how far it has come in recent years, and I know also that the current conditions will help to ensure that this prosperity not decay.[12]

Batista's return to power at the controls of the Cuban state meant a great reordering of affairs, subordinated to the interests of the American Mob. This would have a double character, taking into account that imperialism required a state that was increasingly more efficient. Thus, the dictatorship proceeded toward a greater legalization of the operations of the empire of Havana. A group of state-run or quasi-state-run banking and financial institutions was created for it. In coordination with the international financial center (of more than 50 banks and 200 branches), U.S. Mafia groups and select persons with close ties to the special agencies of the United States, these new institutions might undertake the most fabulous business affairs. The whole enterprise, moreover, could enjoy an increasing cover of legality, by means of a process of gradual transformation of the Cuban economy into a service economy, with a series of special conditions in existence until 1958.

From the beginning, this reordering was helped along by legal advice from U.S. specialists. The organizations that were created in the process would be centralized around General Batista, using his most faithful "yes" men, not only in relation to long-range activities, organized by means of the BNC, but also in projects undertaken by the Banco de Desarrollo Económico y Social or Bank for Economic and Social Development [BANDES].[13] The grand project would also involve multiple schemes instrumented by the Financiera Nacional, the Banco de Comercio Exterior de Cuba, the Banco de Fomento Agrícola e Industrial, Fomento de Hipotecas Aseguradas [FHA], Asociaciones de Créditos and other institutions.

Furthermore, the regime began remodeling Havana, to provide the infrastructure for important business affairs of the Mafia families. This plan included roads connecting important tourist regions, grand avenues, the construction of tunnels and highways, as well as buildings to house the administrative apparatus of a modern state. Among the projects planned was the construction of a great "Plaza of the Republic," dominated by an enormous statue of José Martí. Behind it, a stately Palace of Justice would orchestrate both the fierce repression of popular interests and a climate of absolute flexibility for the dominant groups.

By 1954, the Batista regime had considerably reinforced the scheme of imperialist domination. By carrying out numerous crimes, it had repressed the Centennial Generation, with which Fidel Castro had reinitiated the popular rebellion. Those who had not been assassinated in the Moncada army barracks were imprisoned in the maximum-security jail on the Isla de Pinos. Batista had substantially reinforced the police and military apparatus. The nickel mines had returned to the hands of the powerful Rockefeller group and his allies. The sugar industry had adjusted itself to meet Washington's requirements. Workers or students would protest occasionally, but nothing made the U.S. intelligence community fear that the scheme imposed in Cuba was at any risk.

The head of the CIA (Allen Dulles) visited the Cuban capital at the beginning of 1955 to meet General Batista personally, in the splendid empire of Havana. Two or three months later, Dulles sent an extremely revealing letter. It was headed: Central Intelligence Agency, Washington, D.C., Office of the Director. It was addressed to: His Excellency General Fulgencio Batista Zaldívar, President of the Republic of Cuba, Havana, Cuba. Dated July 15, 1955, it began:

Dear Mr. President,

I remember with great pleasure our meeting held during my trip to Havana last April. For me it was a great honor to have had the pleasurable and interesting experience of visiting you.

The creation by the Cuban Government of the Bureau for Repression of Communist Activities is a great step forward in the cause of liberty. I feel honored that your government has agreed to permit this Agency to assist in the training of some of the officers of this important organization.

As you will remember, in our conversations last April, I established that this agency would feel honored to assist in the training of the personnel that you would send as you wish. I understand that General Martín Díaz Tamayo will direct the activities of the Bureau for Repression of Communist Activities and he will be responsible for its organization. In this case I would like to suggest that it might be advisable for General Díaz Tamayo to come to Washington in the near future, so that we might be able to discuss the activities of international communism. I am sure that it would be useful to exchange opinions with General Díaz Tamayo as a prelude to the group of subordinates who will come here to train. The material we will offer the general could be of considerable help in his task of organizing the Bureau for Repression of Communist Activities. We will indicate to him as well the type of officer that he should prefer upon selecting individuals for training.

In view of the interest that the minister of state, Dr. Carlos Saladrigas, expressed about this matter, I am taking the liberty of writing him today, pointing out to him the ideas contained in this letter. I will suggest to him, if it is acceptable to you and your government, that he extend an invitation in my name to General Díaz Tamayo so that he may come to Washington for approximately two weeks, preferably beginning the August 1. I trust that this will meet with your approval.

Allow me to say again, Mr. President, what a great honor and pleasure it has been to meet and talk with you, and I trust that we will be in a position to assist you and your country in our mutual effort against the enemies of liberty.

Please accept, Mr. President, the renewed declaration of my highest and most distinguished consideration.[14]

It is impossible to carry out an analysis of all the many and varied institutions created by Batista to legalize the business affairs of the Mafia. For this reason, we shall instead offer limited information related to the operations of BANDES [Banco de Desarrollo Económico y Social or Bank for Economic and Social Development].

The idea of creating BANDES emerged in the first days of August 1954 by means of a legal decree, published in an extraordinary issue of the *Gaceta Oficial* on January 27, 1955.[15] In one of its precepts, this law established the fundamental objective of BANDES:

...to facilitate operations of short, medium, and long-range, to carry out a policy of economic and social development, of diversification of production, assuming for that purpose, among others, the functions of discounting and rediscounting public and private securities, issued with the purpose of increasing the money in circulation, as well as realizing as many credit and banking operations as may be indispensable in the realization of such objectives, being authorized to subscribe, float, and endorse bonds of companies of economic and social development — whether state run, quasi state run, or privately run — to make loans to said companies and to issue their own securities.[16]

Such was their financial impunity that Batista himself recognized that, in scarcely four years, institutions like BANFAI, Financiera Nacional, BANDES, Banco de Comercio Exterior de Cuba and others, carried out credit operations totaling almost one billion pesos (equal to the dollar). In reality, these institutions assumed the investments of the financial groups and U.S. Mafia. These funds, given in dollars, were distributed in the following way:

1) For the exploitation of mining, U.S. companies are granted US$76 million.

2) For four (transnational) oil and petrochemical refineries, US$94 million.

3) U.S. electricity (energy production) companies, telephone companies and others received transfers of US$277 million.[17]

Batista also recognized the enormous sum of US$538 million in general investments (at the service of the interests of the Mafia families of Havana or its networks). Of these investments, US$61 million was for the construction of tourist centers, such as hotels and motels. Other amounts include the following: US$20 million for air transportation; US$32 million for railroad transportation and US$96 million for maritime construction. There was almost US$100 million set aside for road infrastructure to Varadero and to the tourist areas of Pinar del Río, plus avenues, tunnels or rejuvenation projects for Havana, preferably in places where the Mafia had or planned new installations. There was US$62 million for buildings to house state agencies, whose objectives were far from the interests of the Cuban nation.

The dictatorship had to maintain a policy of appeasement toward all the forces that formed the real power. It encouraged and assumed foreign investments, besides offering preferential advantages, tax exceptions, gratuities, facilities and guarantees of all kind, which made the U.S. financial groups feel extremely wanted. This policy benefited, to an extraordinary degree, a large number of companies, including Foreign Power (electricity); Firestone Rubber & Tire Company; Dupont Inter-American Chemical Company (paints); Freeport Sulfur Company (nickel and cobalt) and many more.[18]

The reordering of the Cuban economy reached such a scale, that even the U.S. film industry depicted some of its more spectacular excesses. In the film "The Godfather: Part Two," there is a memorable scene set in the presidential palace. In this scene, *mafiosi* and representatives of the financial groups are all sitting at the same table. During the meeting, a famous golden telephone is presented to General Batista by an ITT representative, and passed slowly around the table, much to the envy and admiration of everyone present. The gold phone was presented to the dictator because of the enormous concessions received by the multinational ITT. Amazingly, it was a true story. Studies undertaken by historian Erasmo Dumpierre demonstrate that:

> The institutions of credit and finance, in a true orgy of loans, issued through bonds — printed on state paper — took the cash of banks, security companies and capital banks and savings funds for pensions, retirement and workers' insurance. More than US$900 million was extracted, as follows: BANDES, $500 million; Financiera Nacional, $148 million; Fomento de Hipotecas Aseguradas, $140 million; Banco de Fomento Agrícola, $121 million; Banco Cubano de Comercio Exterior, $48 million; Fondo de Seguro de Depósitos, $10 million.[19]

In addition, there were US$300 million in promissory notes and bonds assigned to interior debt, public debt, exterior debt, etc. The investments with which the criminal state assumed the construction projects of the Mafia and the interests of the U.S. companies would form a very long list.[20]

The regime assumed works at the beach at Varadero. They were valued at US$30 million, creating the Autoridad del Centro Turístico de Varadero [ACETVA], through which the Mafia extended its affairs in an accelerated manner. The many and varied investments and interests included the following:

1) Investments in the Hotel Hilton amounting to more than US$13 million. The Caja de Retiro y Asistencia Social de los Trabajadores Gastronómicos [Savings Fund for Retirement and Social Assistance of Food Industry Workers] was wiped out by the arrangements for a loan of more than US$6 million.

2) US$8 million for a Compania Terminal de Helicópteros. The helicopter station would operate from the flat roof of the building raised on the corner of Obispo and Mercaderes streets (today, it houses the Ministry of Education); and the initiation of flights was projected for November 1958. This company would offer services

between the tourist centers, especially those being constructed or planned for construction on the outskirts of Havana. These included the Monte Carlo de América (today the Marina Hemingway) and areas of Pinar del Río and Varadero. Flights would also link these places with areas of tourist interest in Old Havana.

3) US$13.5 million for a highway construction company.

4) US$5 million for a tourist center in Soroa.

5) US$12 million for the construction of a road link to the Mafia's installations on the beaches to the west of Havana.

6) US$80 million for a project known as Canal Vía Cuba. It would be where the U.S. Government itself possessed strategic interests (a project that would cut Cuba in half) with installations in Cárdenas and to the south of the island in Laguna del Tesoro. The Mafia would operate these new international centers, incorporating drugs, gambling and pornography. Furthermore, new areas to receive contraband and establish highly sought tourism ventures would be opened.

From the very outset, the project would have brought with it unprecedented corruption for the Cuban nation, and it was not attempted because of the great resistance offered by Cubans. The population was not disposed to the country's conversion into the great cesspool of the United States.

Meyer Lansky

Toward the end of 1950, Meyer Lansky decided to move back to Havana. It was the safest place for him and he needed to deal with some disturbing developments there.

Since 1940, his visits in the Cuban capital had been to direct his affairs or carry out inspections, on trips lasting only a few days. Because of the tolerance that had developed for the Mafia in the United States, the bases Lansky favored for directing or coordinating his Cuban interests remained New York, Miami or Las Vegas. The only exception to this was for a few months in 1946 and 1947.

Research has uncovered eyewitness reports from people close to Meyer Lansky. They did not know about all of his many and varied schemes, but were still able to supply valuable information, enabling important conclusions to be made about his role in forming the great Mafia empire in Havana. Meyer Lansky had political connections and contacts with other important *capos*. He was admired and feared by friends and enemies, and nobody had the luxury of ignoring him when important decisions or arrangements were to be made.

In the 1950s, the Mafia considerably expanded its legal activities in Cuba. Lansky continued to operate from the shadows, to tend to these vast interests. His presence in the capital was practically a mystery, in spite of the fact that he was known to various circles of power, including the leadership of the political opposition, senior military officers and executives, as well as to those in the great conglomerates of industry, commerce and finance.

In the early days of the dictatorship, especially in 1954 and 1955, the name Lansky began to be tossed about by journalists. They said he was an important U.S. citizen setting up substantial businesses in Havana. Some still remember the well-known Tendedera, who was given to publicity scandals and, for a certain time, Lansky's radio promoter. Through his broadcasts, Tendedera helped convert the gangster into a kind of benefactor.

Lansky never drank, except on special occasions. The most that he might do to enjoy himself at some gathering was sip a glass of milk. On grand occasions he would make his rounds of the top casinos — maybe the cabaret Montmartre (before the killing of Batista's military intelligence chief, Colonel Blanco Rico), the salons of the Sans Souci in Arroyo Arenas, the scintillating Tropicana or some other famous place. Later, Lansky would ask his assistant to drive his cream-colored convertible Chevrolet slowly through the Malecón area of Havana. He would have the driver stop the car near the old monument to the *U.S.S. Maine* — with that fresh salt air in the early morning hours, only 100 meters from the building occupied by the U.S. embassy. He would stay, breathing the sea breeze without speaking a word, sometimes until the first light of dawn. Lansky also liked the scenery of Quinta Avenida, (Fifth Avenue).

Witnesses agree that this was Lansky's behavior in the months prior to the outbreak of the Mafia war of 1957. No doubt, by this time, many thoughts had emerged during his long and silent reflections on the balcony of his suite at the Hotel Nacional. He was evidently weighing up various possibilities faced by the Havana groups.

On very special occasions, he would ask his assistant to bring him a bottle of pernod, which, it is said, contained a certain amount of opium. Lansky was capable of drinking as much as half a liter, always in silence and in the early morning hours, with the window of his room open. He would be dressed in his underwear (he liked to bathe, sprinkle on talcum powder, and move about his room, always in his underwear) before sitting on that little balcony. He was delighted by the noise of the waves at night.

Witnesses say that Lansky never took notes and never raised his voice, during so many years of dealing with Cuba. He didn't even take the trouble to learn Spanish. He understood the language, but only spoke English. Everybody had to speak to him in English, including Batista.

It is said that, during the 1950s, Lansky did not meet Cubans or visit Cuban families. This is not very credible, if we take into account his complex involvement in the business affairs of the empire of Havana. It is known that he sometimes got rid of his chauffeur-body-guard and drove his Chevrolet convertible himself, spending an evening, perhaps a day or several days, without anyone knowing where he was or what he was doing. It is also known that he used to meet with Batista in the presidential palace itself, and that the meetings could last several hours.

Such was the subordination of the political and military leadership that ruled in Cuba, that the U.S. Mafia felt no respect toward these persons, no matter how high a position they might occupy. There are numerous and well-known anecdotes attesting to this fact. One of these stories concerns events that took place in the grand casino of the Hotel Nacional. It was a night in 1957, when the vice-president of the republic was losing thousands of pesos. He lost all his chips and quickly ran out of cash. He asked the chief of the salon to grant him a credit for 25,000 pesos because he wished to continue playing. It was rather common for this to be done with solvent or prestigious clients. This time, the chief of the salon did not immediately respond. He picked up the telephone and referred the matter to Jack El Cejudo Lansky (Meyer Lansky's brother), who quickly came down to the floor of the salon and, in front of everybody, rudely denied the vice-president the credit he had requested.

Lansky permitted himself the same luxury. According to another story, Lansky once arranged to meet with Amleto Battisti in the Hotel Sevilla Biltmore at 9 p.m. He got out of the car; as always, at the exact hour. As he walked toward the office of the Corsican Mafia boss, he crossed with Santiaguito Rey Pernas, then minister of the interior. Lansky did not even stop. He continued advancing, without greeting the minister, leaving Santiaguito with his hand extended.

It is known that Lansky was married and that his wife resided permanently in the United States, with two daughters. Although Lansky lived an austere life, in order to go unnoticed, he sustained a relationship with a woman of Cuban-European origin for some years. She lived in a second-floor apartment of the Paseo del Prado, which he visited toward the middle of the afternoon, and at times stayed until the next day. The apartment was in the floor above a jeweler's shop, near Refugio Street. The woman was named Carmen; and, after 1959, Lansky sent people from Miami to look for her.

Among the anecdotes that reveal Lansky's personal traits, is one about a long meeting he conducted one night with several of his most important subordinates. After the meeting, he began to make the rounds of the casinos in the grand hotels and cabarets. He had relished his friendly meeting with Harry Smith and Mr. Rosengard, two millionaires, great friends of his, who every now and then landed in Havana to take care of certain affairs. As dawn was breaking, the chauffeur thought Lansky had finished celebrating. But his boss asked the chauffeur to go to one of Marina's houses and bring back two women of the driver's liking.

Marina had several houses, in a chain of specialized brothels servicing luxury hotels. She had a three-story house near the corner of Crespo and Amistad streets, with special rooms, round beds and antique artifacts. There was the El Templo de Marina, next to the Hotel Sevilla Biltmore, right on the corner of the Prado. The "little castle" of Marina was on the corner of the Malecón and Hospital Street. It had 40 permanent women and 300 on file. Within half an hour, any one of these women could be called upon. Marina had another brothel in a building on San José Street, and a chain of lingerie shops on the Prado.

That night, the chauffeur drove toward another famous brothel, also one of Marina's, at the intersection of Ferrocarril and Boyeros. Lansky's chauffeur thought the old man had requested two women for himself. Yet when he returned, the driver was surprised. After drinking a half bottle of pernod, Lansky told the chauffeur he could take one of the women to his room. Lansky would take the other.

Lansky organized his business affairs efficiently, meeting his staff once a week. It could be on a Thursday or a Friday, from 2 p.m. until 5 p.m., following a strictly punctual routine. The meetings themselves took place at Joe Stasi's house.

At that time (prior to the Mafia war of 1957) the leading staff members of the U.S. Mafia in Cuba were as follows: Joe Stasi, Mr. Normain, Santo Trafficante Jr. and Lansky himself, the creator and chief of the empire of Havana. In general, all the Mafia families of Havana were subordinate to that structure.

Rigorous security measures were enforced for staff meetings. Almost nobody knew about them. Mr. Normain, Joe Stasi, Trafficante Jr. and Lansky went to Stasi's residence on the other side of the Almendares River. The house was set in a wooded area, on the zig-zagging 47th Avenue, No. 1405.

Joe Stasi was general manager for all Mafia business affairs in Cuba. Mr. Normain constituted a kind of itinerant controller of organized gambling, casinos, high-class prostitution and many other interests based in the interior of the country. Santo Trafficante Jr. was Lansky's deputy, personally responsible for drug (cocaine) channels and trafficking, which brought in hundreds of millions of dollars. Santo's father, Santo Trafficante Snr. was also a deputy of Lansky's.

Relations among the Mafia families of Havana were not always harmonious. Barletta's ties with "legal" business made him a personal friend of the president. However, the interests of the Corsican Amleto Battisti y Lora (who was the bridge to Luciano's heroin channels) were not handled directly by the dictator, but through Lansky. Amleto's activities had a well-defined ceiling. In spite of this, Amleto allowed himself some independence. To gain an idea of the power of the key *mafiosi* and the relationships they enjoyed, suffice it to say that Amleto could always slip into the Cuban Congress, occupying a Liberal Party seat in the house of representatives, thanks to the flexibility of the Suárez Rivas brothers.

Lansky always took charge of sensitive or complicated matters, acting from the shadows. His brief included finances, politics and contacts with prestigious lawyers, legal advisers and influential personalities in Cuba and the United States. As has already been said, seen in the modern sense, the empire of Havana resembled a giant corporation, with various departments and divisions.

Toward the middle of 1956, Lansky stayed a few days in Varadero in the company of Harry Smith. Two days later, Mr. Rosengard joined them. The three spent the day together, seated on the porch of a mansion or walking along the seashore. Rosengard was known as a cultured man and belonged to a prestigious Boston society family. Smith, for his part, had devoted himself to mining and had hotel interests in the United States and Canada.

Harry Smith was no stranger to Havana. The magazine *Havana Chronicle*, published by the Comisión Nacional de Turismo de Cuba (two issues apeared in 1941 and 1942) listed him at that time as president of the Jockey Club in the Havana race track. Furthermore, he was an executive in the Panama Pacific Line Company, which had offices in the Lonja del Comercio. The maritime company operated ships that made regular trips to the Far East, with stops in the port of Havana. The most important thing in this story is that we have found a receipt for rental of Safety Deposit Box No. 163 in the bank The Trust Company of Cuba, to which only three people had access: Harry Smith, Meyer Lansky, and J. E. Rosengard.

Slim and small in stature, Lansky dressed in expensive but conventional clothes, perfectly in tune with the aspirations of a man who wanted to go unnoticed. On his right hand, however, he wore a star sapphire, mounted in platinum; on his left wrist, an extraflat watch with platinum casing and a velvet band. Lansky used English cologne and shaved exclusively with Gillette razors. He never wore a hat in Cuba. His favorite expression, repeated to people closest to him, was that one always had to be careful. The best thing was to be inconspicuous. Lansky had a luxury suite on the 10th floor of the Hotel Riviera, reserved exclusively for special meetings. Of all Cuban music, he felt a special predilection for the *danzón*.

In recent years, U.S. books and films have portrayed Meyer Lansky's presence in Havana, sometimes just in passing, at other times transforming history into myth. The makers of the movie "Havana" tried to reconstruct the period — albeit poorly — and went far beyond the usual passing glance. They presented Meyer

Lansky as a character actually exercising the mechanisms of power against the destiny of the Cuban nation. This is especially true of a scene in which a professional gambler waits with Lansky's deputy (a role possibly inspired by Joe Stasi, called Joe Volpi in the movie). In the scene, the gambler is finally to be received by Lansky. A door opens, but the "Mafia financier" ignores the gambler completely and speaks to Joe. The following dialogue ensues:

> MEYER LANSKY: Where's the fuckin' offensive I paid for?
>
> JOE VOLPI: Well, there's supposed to be an armored train.
>
> MEYER LANSKY: Oh, an armored train. Like China, like Siberia, like the Boxer fuckin' Rebellion.
>
> JOE VOLPI: They promised…
>
> MEYER LANSKY: You shut up and listen to me. Now here's what you do tomorrow. You're gonna go to Batista's people and you're gonna talk to them and you're gonna explain to them how upset I am. You're gonna tell them they better get off their asses and start fighting pretty soon or they're gonna go back to bein' a bunch of fuckin' banana eaters like they used to be. You're gonna remind them that the only reason that there's civilized plumbing in this country is because the Americans came here in '98 and beat the shit out of Spain. Batista's own palace had a fuckin' outdoor crapper before we put one inside. Now the only reason he's got an army is because we gave him one. Well he better start using it or he's gonna wind up on some street corner selling beans like he started. We invented Havana, and we can goddamn well move it someplace else if he can't control it. Now you explain that to him.[1]

From April to October of 1958, Lansky made quick, brief and continuous trips to other places in the Caribbean — the Dominican Republic, Martinique, Barbados, Puerto Rico, Trinidad, Tobago, Jamaica and the Bahamas. This was to expand his business affairs, especially in new hotel-casinos tied to international tourism. These events correspond with the preoccupations he would have naturally felt because of fast-changing events on the island. However, it is certain that, as of October 1958, he did not leave Cuba — until January 2 or 3, 1959.

According to our sources, Lansky stayed in Havana to make sure Batista resisted the desperate maneuvers that Washington had begun to implement in the new circumstances. These measures led inevitably to the end of the monopoly the Mafia families had enjoyed in Havana, in the great business affairs facilitated by the criminal state in Cuba.

Following Batista's exit from power, inevitable changes were made to manipulate or neutralize the victorious march of the Cuban Revolution. They made possible the entrance into Cuba of rival Mafia forces, with which the Havana groups had maintained a nagging dispute for so long. These rival factions of the U.S. Mafia felt they should also participate in the fabulous profits reported by the empire of Havana.

Our research shows that Meyer Lansky returned to the Cuban capital during the first half of March, 1959. He stayed a little less than a week, in his favorite suite in the Hotel Nacional. After making some deals, he declared that, unfortunately for him, a revolution was beginning whose purpose was to strip the rich of their wealth and redistribute it to the poorest people in the country. Thus, he had nothing more to do in Cuba.

Mafia War in Havana

Lansky was convinced that war with the New York Mafia groups was inevitable, and began to take a series of measures. The first of these, toward the end of 1956, was to pretend that he was retiring, then to create in Havana a typical Mafia syndicate that would pass to the direction of Santo Trafficante Jr. Lansky initiated a series of alliances with like-minded elements from Las Vegas, Chicago and California. He made arrangements with important politicians and financiers, besides strengthening his old ties with the intelligence services, to ensure business affairs in Cuba were put on more solid foundations.

Interests represented by Sam Giancana from Chicago began to operate in Cuba. The brothers Joe and Charlie Sileci also settled in Havana. Numerous Italian American gangsters, along with stellar figures of the Hollywood movie industry who were tied to Mafia families — such as Tony Martin, Donald O'Connor, Frank Sinatra and George Raft — also appeared in Havana. A select group of U.S. businessmen helped to establish links with great political influences, including the White House itself.[1] Similarly, Nick de Constance (Nicholas de Constanzo) settled in the Cuban capital. Known as the "Fat Butcher," Constanzo was an extraordinarily feared man and would soon assume control all of Havana's casinos. Here, we should note two interesting documents: applications sent to the

Gabinete Nacional de Identificación, for the granting of foreigner's identification cards. The Fat Butcher appears with the number 396315; and Joe Sileci with number 396316. Both transactions (to legalize their residence status in Cuba) were processed together.[2] People who knew him say that Nicholas de Constanzo was almost two meters (six feet, seven inches) tall.[3] Several times, they saw him grasp other *mafiosi* by the lapels of their jackets, picking them up with one hand, before plastering them against a wall at the Hotel Capri or Hotel Riviera.

With the new arrangements in place, Jack El Cejudo Lansky began to direct the Hotel Nacional.[4] Meanwhile, Willberg Clark controlled multiple affairs in Varadero. Charles Wife, for his part, known as Navajita, was in charge of the casino of the Hotel Internacional de Varadero. Navajita had a luxurious apartment in the floor above Club 21, on the corner of 21st and N Streets, in Vedado.

The Fat Butcher established his operational headquarters in the Hotel Capri. Although the Capri boasted the stellar presence of George Raft, the latter did not really have as much power as it seemed. It is known that he had run into some difficulties with the Mafia in the United States, but both he and the crime organization had sought reconciliation. Raft was something of a manager. His role was to be the host of millionaire U.S. citizens invited to Havana for a weekend, or for a stay of a week or two, with all expenses paid: rooms, drinks, meals, women, drugs or other indulgences. All these amenities served to lure the wealthy world to Havana, with the expectation that each guest would leave several thousand dollars as he or she passed through the gaming parlors.

The Pertierra family (who also managed the famous El Monseñor restaurant) ran the luxurious Havana cabaret Montmartre, under the charge of Amadeo Barletta. The Montmartre was a few steps from the street known as La Rampa. In 1956, a revolutionary commando executed Batista's chief of military intelligence, Colonel Blanco Rico, in the Montmartre, and the Mafia considered it an opportune time to close the place.

Affairs in the Hotel Deauville continued to be conducted directly by Santo Trafficante Jr. and several important Italian American *mafiosi*.[5] In addition, Evaristo Fernández was employed as a "visible head" of power. All these people had long-standing ties with the Cosa Nostra.

To control the multiple interests of the Parisien cabaret, the Italian American gangster Eddy Cheeline was put in charge. Thus, the grand casino in the Hotel Habana Hilton passed to the control of Raúl González Jerez,[6] who had directed important affairs, including interests in the Havana race track. To manage the casino in the Havana Hilton and similar businesses, however, a kind of Cuban American company was created. This was simply a front; many U.S. *mafiosi* were installed in the Havana Hilton, which also housed the operational headquarters of Joseph Luigi Sileci.

A gangster known as Tower ran the casino of the Hotel Plaza, near Central Park; where the first of Havana's schools for dealers was immediately set up on the building's flat roof. These training schools were for teaching the techniques of various forms of gambling, not just to meet demands for new staff in the empire of Havana, but for training people to work in other parts of the Caribbean, and in capital cities of the Americas and the United States.

The schools were created by the highly experienced Milton Saide, who organized a second school in the Sans Souci cabaret.[7] A third school was established in the building of Ambar Motors, in the middle of La Rampa of Havana. Later — so great was the expansion — a fourth school also operated in the Odontológico Building, under the charge of Tommy Ransoni. When these schools were functioning to perfection, Milton Saide began to direct multiple operations from the Hotel Capri, where he was installed as a boss.

There were many other casinos in Greater Havana, operating in cabarets such as the Sans Souci (where there were two gaming areas) and in the Tropicana and other famous nightspots. There were also important casinos and gambling parlors in the Hotel Nacional, the Hotel Capri, the Hotel Riviera and Hotel Deauville (where there were two casinos). There were casinos in the Hotel Habana Hilton and Hotel Sevilla Biltmore. The grand Casino Nacional was across from Central Park. There were also casinos in the Hotel Plaza, the Hotel Internacional de Varadero and Hotel St. John. There were casinos in almost all the large cities in the interior of the island, including the cabaret Venecia in Santa Clara, the motel Jagua in Cienfuegos and gambling parlors of the famous Castillo del Valle. Other casinos of a more popular nature were found in key locations in the nocturnal world of the capital, such as the Barrio Chino (Chinese Quarter). There was a casino across from the funeral home on Zanja Street, one at Cuatro Caminos and other gaming parlors in different parts of town; or in places of recreation, such as the installations of the Jockey Club and the cabaret Alibar. The list would be too long to mention them all.

Because of the confidence he enjoyed, Joe Stasi continued to direct everything related to gambling in Cuba. It was said of Stasi that in the middle of a meeting he was capable of falling asleep or pretending to fall asleep, only to wake up at precisely the appropriate moment and join in the discussion with absolute coherence.

Mr. Normain continued to administer his control in the interior of the country. Normain was the husband of the singer Olga Chaviano. The pair had an elegant apartment, which Normain never used, in the Focsa building. When he was away making his rounds, and especially when he was gone from Havana for a few days, Olga devoted herself to steamy dalliances. The scandals were famous.

Throughout 1956 and almost all of 1957, the New York Mafia groups and others (Genovese, Anastasia, Profaci, Gambino, et al.) continued with their plans to set up in Havana. This was thought necessary because congressional proceedings carried out in the United States meant U.S. Mafia activities there were being exposed or investigated. The multiple links between business, politics and crime were being examined. Meanwhile, the imperialist scheme imposed in Cuba offered absolute impunity to the Mafia. More than just giving guarantees, this scheme had completely legalized the Mafia's big business affairs.

By 1956, the rival Mafia groups knew of the project to construct a chain of hotels over the entire northern extremity of the provinces of Havana and Matanzas, including Havana's Malecón, converting the area into a paradise for moneyed tourism from the United States.

The development of supersonic aviation put Havana in an extremely privileged position, allowing easy access to the empire of gambling, drugs and sex. The Mafia knew that, by 1959, the island was only three or four hours from principal U.S. cities. Although the network of air links with Cuba was already quite vast, the introduction of supersonic commercial flights meant the elite of the business world would come under the influence of the Mafia empire of Havana.[8]

After having exhausted all means of obtaining entry to Havana — petitions, supplications, influences and pressures — the New York groups simply forced their way in, by installing some casinos in Cuba, in the first months of 1957.

By then, Meyer Lansky had a new strategy. He pretended to have retired from his business affairs. In fact, he was still directing them from the shadows. He was pulling strings, maintaining his ties with political groups in Washington and the intelligence services. His plan was not just to resist the New York and other rival Mafia groups, but to launch a grand-scale offensive against them.

When the Mafia war fought over access to Cuba finally erupted, it was a quick and violent conflict. The power of the Mafia families in Havana, and the degree to which their interests were bound up with U.S. power groups, was made only too apparent. The fray did not develop on the island. Rather, the Mafia families of Havana carried the conflict over to U.S. territory, and with such deadly efficiency that the New York groups were obliged to seek a hasty peace.

The dispute left many dead in the principal cities of the United States. Anastasia was dead. Scalise, intimate friend of Luciano, was killed. After the uproarious attempted murder of Frank Costello, which attracted much unwanted publicity, the New York Mafia families had no alternative but to urgently convoke the famous Appalachian meeting, which took place on November 14, 1947. In Havana, meanwhile, U.S. intelligence tried to stabilize the criminal state in crisis, as the Rebel Army stepped up its military operations.

In his book, *Brotherhood of Evil: The Mafia,* Frederic Sondern Jr., a senior official of the U.S. Narcotics Department, affirms:

> A number of emergencies had arisen [refering to the Mafia war in the United States over the territory of Cuba] which particularly concerned the *mafiosi* of New York and the eastern seaboard. During recent months

rivalries and violent disputes between powerful brethren had led to the unfortunately sensational assassinations of Francesco Scalici and Umberto Anastasio, the attempted murder of Francesco Castiglia [Frank Costello], and the killing of several less important members. The traditional unity and discipline within the society were being shaken, the elders felt, and stricter lines of jurisdictional demarcation in the narcotics, gambling and labor fields had to be drawn at once. There were other serious problems. Ever since the Kefauver and the Daniels Committees of the U.S. Senate were thoroughly shocked some years ago by the testimony of Treasury Department agents concerning the Mafia's structure and its role in organized crime, congress has become increasingly concerned with what formerly seemed a myth to most of the legislators. The prying of Senator McClellan's more recently constituted Antirackets Committee [in mid-1958] had grown embarrassing.[9] National magazines and many newspapers had given the brotherhood much unwanted publicity.[10]

The meeting that the U.S. Mafia convoked for November 14, 1957, which was held in southern New York, marked the crucial point of the defeat of the enemies of Meyer Lansky.

The Appalachian meeting was really a failure. Luciano and Adonis could not attend (they were in Italy) although Luciano sent a message. Costello (after the attempt on his life) felt that he had nothing to talk about, or he simply knew that the gathering was doomed. Umberto Anastasio and Scalise were cadavers. Lansky, in mid-1956, had announced his retirement; and, of course, in keeping with his strategy, kept watch from the sidelines. Lansky had such foresight that (according to his chauffeurs' testimony),[11] leaving his Friday afternoon meetings at Joe Stasi's house, he acted on various occasions as though he really was disgusted by the actions and ideas of Santo Trafficante Jr.

Nevertheless, almost all the groups with designs on Cuba attended the Appalachian meeting of November 14, 1957, held in southern New York. As Frederic Sondern writes:

Among those present were 19 delegates from upstate New York, 23 from New York City and adjacent New Jersey area, eight from the Midwest, three from beyond the Rocky Mountains, two from the South, two from Cuba, one from Italy.[12]

The Mafia families that operated in the United States claimed that they had faced constant threats since the early 1950s, because of the revelations of the Kefauver Commission of 1950-52. Investigations of the (1955) Daniels Commission into narcotics trafficking also seriously affected the principal sources of income of the Mafia families in the United States.

The disastrous Appalachian meeting then gave way to the investigations of another U.S. Senate commission presided over by Senator John McClellan (who directed the Commission on Illegal Activities in Labor and Management). The Mafia crisis also resulted in the activities of the then Senator Robert Kennedy, but all these efforts to uncover Mafia influence would be "diluted" as part of a wider historic process within the United States.

In Havana, however, it was a different story. The U.S. economic and political system passed through a process of internal struggle after revelations about the Mafia had emerged, but U.S. imperialism had made the island a paradise of Mafia impunity, while simultaneously and brutally repressing popular Cuban interests.

At the Appalachian meeting, two people represented the empire of Havana: Santo Trafficante Jr. and Joe Sileci. The former attended in his apparent capacity as chief of the *mafiosi* groups in Cuba, while Joe Sileci represented the new alliances.

It is certain that beginning with Lansky's supposed "retirement," the general structure of the Mafia rule in Havana had changed. It was no longer characterized by those famous meetings between Normain, Stasi, Trafficante Jr. and Meyer Lansky in Stasi's wooded residence on the Almendares River. Now, almost all affairs (which were previously operated by visible Creole heads) were run directly by U.S. *mafiosi*.

The following quote, from Frederic Sondern, is necessarily extensive, because of the historic circumstances to which it refers. (Neither Frederic Sondern Jr., in 1958, nor Mario Puzo, in his novel, *The Godfather*, could resist offering visions of what was happening to Mafia affairs in Cuba.)

> Another issue which had aroused intense debate at Barbara's [a reference to the Appalachian meeting][13] concerned jurisdiction in the enormously

lucrative gambling operation which has mushroomed in Cuba during the last two years and is beginning to surpass even that of Las Vegas. Luigi Santo Trafficante and a partner, Joe Sileci, had come from Havana to establish before the *capi mafiosi* their exclusive overlordship, of long standing, in this domain... Trafficante... and associates had set up a typical syndicate... His political connections were formidable, reaching well into President Batista's palace. All was legal; no police could interfere; it was a racketeer's dream of legitimacy and security come true. Suddenly his position was threatened by a fellow *mafioso*. Umberto (Albert) Anastasio, one of the extremely wealthy and powerful masters of the docks and numbers rackets in New York, was sending agents to Cuba to scout for projects — without Trafficante's permission. This was a serious breach of the brotherhood's rules, and complaints went promptly from Havana to New York. Anastasio was apparently warned by other *capi mafiosi*, but kept right on with his predatory plans. As a result, on October 25, 1957, Umberto was shot expertly through the head by two calm executioners as he sat in a barber chair in the Sheraton Park Hotel, in midtown Manhattan. The case, like most Mafia assassinations, has not been solved. Trafficante and Sileci had been bothered by the New York police about Anastasio's murder, and Sileci subsequently sent a message [from Havana][14] to District Attorney Hogan, who wanted him for questioning, to "drop dead." Now they wished assurances from the elders that such invasions and embarrassments would not occur again.[15]

Havana's Mafia families reported the Appalachian meeting to the New York Police. All the *mafiosi* were rounded up, arrested, interrogated and booked: something very frightening for the New York groups.

Arrangements made by Lansky led to the arrest, trial and conviction of Vito Genovese. As part of this inter-Mafia war, the Havana groups also coordinated the dismantling of one of the rival family's most important networks for the trafficking and distribution of narcotics. Forty gangsters were imprisoned. Stromberg was the main "visible head" to be incarcerated. It is a curious fact that almost all the evidence the U.S. police needed to carry out this operation on U.S. soil was supplied by the Cuban intelligence services.

The Empire's **11** Last Stand

By March 1958, the U.S. Mafia was helping to organize the grand offensive of Batista's army against Fidel Castro's guerrillas. It was also mounting a grand offensive of its own. It was rapidly organizing the construction of a highly ambitious and extensive hotel complex. This complex would be known as the Hotel Monte Carlo de La Habana, and built in the area of Santa Fe, in Barlovento, to the west of Havana, 25 minutes from the Capitol building.[1]

According to documentation, the Monte Carlo de La Habana (now the Marina Hemingway) was to be the first huge, resort-like hotel complex constructed in the world. It was to have 656 rooms, in a vast complex that included a grand casino for millionaire tourists, with an ostentatious cabaret, a pier, docks and interior canals for yachts. It would also have golf courses, and various other installations,[2] at a cost of more that US$20 million, with financing to be assumed substantially by BANDES.

The most astonishing thing about the project was the list of people associated with its operation. Together with known *mafiosi* were names that enjoyed a certain prestige in the United States. As documents of the day reveal, in order to undertake the project the U.S. Mafia formed a front company called Compañía Hotelera del Oeste.[3] In a letter from BANDES addressed to Julio Lobo's Banco Financiero (August 16, 1956), there is discussion of a Hotel Monaco

— with mention of an initial sum of US$12 million.[4] (We presume that this project later became the Monte Carlo.) Such operations and plans were expressions of an accelerated interweaving of interests of the financial-Mafia-intelligence services groups, not just in Cuba but in the United States itself.

The Compañía Hotelera del Oeste was in charge of construction of the hotel complex and, to direct its operations, the Mafia designated Manuel Santeiro Jr., (connected with the Toledo sugar mill), the architect Serafín Leal Otaño and lawyer Virgilio Villar Gil. Manuel Santeiro Jr. was a well-known businessman and director of the Central Fajardo and Güines sugar companies; attorney for the family interests of Manuel Aspuru and treasurer of the Compañía Licorera de Cuba. He was also a famous "club man" in Havana society.[5]

For its part, the company that would operate the Monte Carlo (after the hotel was constructed) had already been constituted by Public Deed No. 221, on August 15, 1957. It was located on Obispo Street, No. 104, on the fifth floor. This deed was signed in the presence of the notary public Jose Berruf y Jiménez, on behalf of Dr. Jorge S. Casteleiro y Colmenares.[6]

Of the stockholders and representatives of the U.S. Mafia in the Compañía de Hotel Monte Carlo, sources reveal that its president was William Miller, of Miami, Florida. For more than 14 years, Miller had run the most successful restaurant in the world, the Bill Miller Riviera, in New York City, making it a very profitable concern. Furthermore, he had undertaken big deals in Las Vegas, especially in the Hotel Sahara.[7]

Another president of the board of directors of Hotel Monte Carlo de La Habana was the famous Frank Sinatra, a leading artist and producer of important network television programs in the United States. Sinatra ran his own movie company, and planned to use the assets from the Hotel Monte Carlo de La Habana to transmit television programs weekly to the United States.

Reports the Mafia groups sent to BANDES say Sinatra was also a successful man in aviation companies, including Capitol Airlines and TWA. He was involved with important transportation and publicity companies and co-owner of the Hotel Sands in Las Vegas, "which is public and notorious, and the most successful in the area."[8]

Walter Kirschner was director of the Monte Carlo de La Habana. He had lived in the White House for 12 years as President Roosevelt's adviser.[9] It was said of Kirschner:

> Currently [1958]... he enjoys the privilege of being able to have an audience with the president [a reference to Eisenhower] in his residence, owing to his personal friendship and as a man capable of representing the interests of the state because of his having done so on previous occasions, for example, in Vatican City, where he was the first envoy of the government of his country.[10]

The name Kirschner appears in books written about President Roosevelt and in the presidential memoirs of Truman.

Another director of the board of stockholders of the Hotel Monte Carlo de La Habana was Alfred Dicker, of Washington, D.C., one of the most prestigious builders of highways in the United States. Yet another director was the well-known movie star, Tony Martin, of Los Angeles, California, who was also a producer of television and radio programs, movies and records. Martin, who was a successful man, seemed tied to diverse interests of the U.S. Mafia. He was co-owner of the Hotel Flamingo, one of the most important Mafia centers in Las Vegas, which was also used for filming movies.

Another director of Monte Carlo de La Habana was the movie actor Donald O'Connor. O'Connor was one of the youngest movie producers in Hollywood and had been a star since the age of 21, when he began working with Bing Crosby. He had great influence in television and radio programming in the United States, and owned his own movie company.[11] Among the directors of the Hotel Monte Carlo de La Habana was I. Blacker, of Miami, Florida, the visible owner and operator of the hotels Sans Souci, Deauville and Sherry Fonternac.

Another was Samuel Edelman, of New York City, operator of large real estate companies in New York. Edelman ran some of the largest office buildings in that city, and had many other investments. Yet another director was Edward Marshall of Englewood, a lawyer and famous financier from New York, with significant interests in the Acceptance Finance Company. He was also director of Marshall Plan Finance.

As one can see, the group of U.S. citizens who were to operate the Hotel Monte Carlo de La Habana had great experience in networking and deal-making. They had been, or were currently, directors of companies, or had been majority operators in the hotels Casa Blanca, Deauville, Sans Souci, Sherry Fonternac and Versailles, all in Miami; and the hotels Flamingo, Sahara and Sands in Las Vegas. All these hotels were tied to the Mafia.

The operations to be undertaken by the Hotel Monte Carlo de La Habana depended on the absolute backing of Meyer Lansky. It is not surprising, therefore, that various institutions are implicated in the surviving documents that made the deal legal (those that were not destroyed). These institutions include: BANDES, Financiera Nacional, Banco de Comercio Exterior de Cuba, Julio Lobo's Banco Financiero, BNC, the Compañía Hotelera La Riviera de Cuba and other official or private entities linked with groups or companies of the Mafia.

All the Mafia's projects in Cuba at the end of the 1950s were somehow linked to the Compañía Hotelera La Riviera de Cuba. Links with companies or financial groups for the construction of grand hotel-casinos, and related or peripheral businesses, reaffirm the appropriateness of Meyer Lansky's international title as the "financier of the Mafia."

The construction of the Monte Carlo de La Habana hotel complex fell to the Compañía Hotelera del Oeste. After the hotel's inauguration, the complex would pass to the control of the Compañía Monte Carlo. The most significant thing about this deal, however, was the fact that it allowed a much wider objective to be pursued by the Mafia. The hotel would initiate a new era; a series of large-scale and ambitious Mafia projects would begin in Cuba. The Monte Carlo de La Habana project would begin to reinforce, stabilize and enhance the image of the Cuban (criminal) state, both in the United States and the rest of the world. The new image would be used to win over public opinion. This was thought necessary, because the scheme of domination imposed on Cuba was being thrown into crisis as the Rebel Army carried out its war operations from the Sierra Maestra mountains.

Furthermore, surviving documents point out that, in regard to those directing the operation of the Hotel Monte Carlo, and especially Mr. Miller, Frank Sinatra, Donald O'Connor and Tony Martin:

They have at their disposal the best executive managers in the United States. Mr. Miller is considered within the United States as the only person capable of what Americans call raising the dead. In other words, he has long experience staging shows that are huge tourist attractions in the United States, and he has contacts and connections with first-rate U.S. artistic businesses. As a guarantee, he has offered *to bring to Cuba the 20 most important stars in the United States to promote international publicity in favor of the government directed by Major General Fulgencio Batista y Zaldívar.*[12] He is the person who will be in charge of the operation of the Hotel Monte Carlo de La Habana.[13]

In relation to Tony Martin, O'Connor and Frank Sinatra, it is made clear that:

[Frank Sinatra][14] wants to televise the hotel's properties from Cuba to the United States weekly, given that he as producer and as an interested party in his programs intends to fulfill a double function: first, to put the hotel he manages in the spotlight; and second, to divert the profits produced by contracting the show in Cuba to a Cuban American [read Mafia front][15] company that will produce shows and movies from Cuba with panoramic vistas of the hotel serving as a backdrop.[16]

At this time, the forces acting against the Cuban nation were of such magnitude that, in a letter of May 14, 1958, Jesús M. Otero, administrator of the law firm Beguiristaín-Quezada, wrote the president of BANDES, requesting absolute discretion in the operation that the Mafia was setting up in Havana:

[Those] interested in the operation and construction of the Hotel Monte Carlo de La Habana have projected a vast plan of international publicity… based primarily on the publicity value of the names of some members of the company known around the world because of their activities in film, radio and television… We think that the publicity effect that we are pursuing would be accomplished by leaking to the public those names, contrary to the arranged plan, for which the customary secrecy is advisable… We can assure that our publicity plan… can be calculated at a cost of not less than US$3 million."[17]

Revolution in Cuba 12

The U.S. president, Dwight D. Eisenhower, tells us in his memoirs that:

> Throughout 1958, in accordance with the Charter of the OAS, the United States carefully followed a policy of nonintervention in Cuba, although popular support for Castro was widespread. We repeatedly seized cargoes of arms headed for Castro and in March suspended the delivery of arms to Batista.[1]

This statement does not withstand the slightest comparison with historical fact. After March 1958, and until the final days of the revolutionary war, Batista continued to receive arms, supplies and material resources through a range of channels. He continued to receive the support of U.S. politicians and intelligence agencies. The training of the dictatorship's troops continued to be advised by a military delegation from the United States established in Cuba. Above all, the intelligence services operations became bolder and more intense. When Batista's planes systematically bombed vast rural regions in the former province of Oriente, the dictator's air force was supplied from the very arsenals of the U.S. naval base at Guantánamo.

In September 1958 the inspector general of the CIA, Lyman Kirkpatrick, made his last trip to Havana. He held meetings with the chief of the CIA based in Havana, and with advisers, military attaches, representatives of the FBI, bureaucrats, intelligence agents, financiers, executives of U.S. companies, the political leadership of the U.S. embassy and other agents and private figures and officials. He reached the conclusion (according to statements he made 10 years later) that Batista had lost control of the country, and the only hope rested in a miracle.[2]

Everything seems to indicate, however, that until October 1958, the U.S. financial groups, the Mafia and intelligence services maintained a coherent political agenda without too many cracks developing. This was not all that surprising, given the extraordinary profits reported by Batista. Any fissures sprang from characteristics peculiar to each of these forces, or from the hypocritical maneuvers undertaken by U.S. State Department to maintain Batista as head of the government.

In the first days of November 1958 the cohesion was shattered, and each of the three forces assumed a position consistent with its own particular interests. The situation had entered an acute crisis because the island was in a state of insurrection from one end to the other. Nobody could stop the revolutionary movement directed by Fidel Castro. Without a doubt, U.S. intelligence specialists had reached their own conclusions much earlier, especially by the end of July 1958, when the 300 guerrillas in the Sierra Maestra defeated the 10,000 soldiers of the dictatorship. Such were the ties between the U.S. financial-Mafia-intelligence groups, however, that they maintained a joint effort to ensure continuity of their domination over Cuba.

In the first days of November, combat began in the outskirts of Guisa. Fidel Castro, from the battleground, directed his forces against the tanks and airplanes, just nine kilometers from the command post of the elite troops of the dictatorship.

Batista's troops were defeated by the Rebel Army, a truly heroic feat. That was when the powerful U.S. intelligence community established in Havana was persuaded that nothing could stop the rebel forces.

In the first days of November 1958 the CIA felt compelled to inform President Eisenhower of this serious new danger to U.S. influence over Cuba.[3] This was also most likely when the CIA first considered ridding themselves of Batista.

This measure, proposed in November, became for the U.S. Government a truly sticky affair. It never imagined that, following express orders from the Mafia families established in Cuba, Batista would dare to resist Washington's plans. Batista's unwillingness obliged the U.S. Government to seek a new option by which the old scheme could be maintained, even if this meant a military solution; albeit one involving the variables of the electoral farce of November 1958.

The reason the U.S. Mafia groups in Havana resisted Washington is clear. Without Batista, or his political-military leadership, they could not prevent the entrance into Cuba of the powerful New York Mafia families with whom they had been at war in 1957, or prevent the dispersion of their lucrative business deals in Havana.

Washington made clear to the dictator that he would have to rapidly abandon the country, along with his family. He could settle again in Daytona Beach, with the understanding that his interests, and the interests of his friends, would be protected.

Batista had US$300 million in banks outside Cuba. Why wouldn't he accept Washington's generous offer, with the revolutionary troops quickly advancing toward the western part of the country? Nevertheless, against all predictions, he refused Washington's proposal.

Everything indicates that the Mafia families of Havana did not trust the offer, and began to pressure their connections, lobbying interested parties for a negotiated solution or military intervention.

It is now known that a four-motor DC-6B, on a special National Airlines flight, landed at the international airport of Rancho Boyeros, on December 9, 1958. It carried a secret emissary of the U.S. Government, William D. Pawley, who was already known in Cuba. Pawley was a very experienced former official in the U.S. State Department. He had been ambassador to Peru and Brazil, besides having multiple connections with business, politics and organized crime.

Penny Lernoux, in one of her research studies of banks and the U.S. Mafia, links Pawley with that shadowy world:

As in Southeast Asia, right-wing politics forged an alliance in southern Florida between the CIA and organized crime. In 1960, when the CIA was devising plots to eliminate Castro, it used a contract agent, Robert Maheu, to contact the mobster John Roselli. [In the United States the rumor continues to be spread that the Mafia was contracted to assassinate Fidel Castro. This rumor's purpose was to cover up the true dimensions of the Mafia in U.S. society. The Mafia in the United States, unlike in Cuba at the time, was not a marginal group. Rather, it was one with real power and, as such, did not have to be contracted, especially given that it had just lost its splendid empire of Havana].[4] John Roselli in turn introduced Maheu to Trafficante and to Sam Giancana, the Chicago *capo*. During a 1961 meeting at Miami's Hotel Fontainebleau, Maheu gave Trafficante and Roselli poison capsules to be smuggled into Cuba to kill Castro, but the attempt failed. Two years later Trafficante was again involved with the CIA in a bizarre boat raid against Cuba cosponsored by William Pawley, a former assistant secretary of state and wealthy financier who had been a colleague of Paul Helliwell's in China and was co-founder of the Flying Tigers, later a CIA airline known as Civil Air Transport, involved in arms smuggling in the Far East. Pawley also participated in the CIA coup against the Arbenz Government in Guatemala in 1954, along with another Helliwell associate.[5]

Pawley's colleague (Helliwell) was a lawyer and banker in Miami, and the chief of special information in China during World War II for the OSS, precursor of the CIA. He undertook innumerable activities associated with the CIA and the Mafia. Furthermore, Helliwell payrolled the CIA's affairs in Florida connected with the Bay of Pigs invasion. He manipulated numerous banks in the southern United States, and in parts of the Caribbean and Bahamas, that facilitated CIA operations and laundered dollars for the U.S. Mafia. Helliwell was the "head of the prestigious Miami law firm of Helliwell, Melrose and DeWolf."[6]

At the end of 1958, William D. Pawley arrived in Havana to hold a secret meeting with General Batista and communicate Washington's proposal, which the general could not refuse under any circumstances, or so it was supposed. Pawley was one of the people responsible for dismantling Havana's trolley system. In a masterful maneuver, urban transportation in all the important Cuban cities became dependent on the automobile industry of the United States. Of course, the U.S. Mafia possessed interests in this industry, and control over the distribution of automobiles and parts, both in Cuba and the United States.

For decades, expertise and cash had been invested in the construction of Havana's trolley system. This service was more economical than one based on the automobile. Nevertheless, by 1950, transportation in the largest cities of Cuba became entirely dependent upon the importation of vehicles and increasingly expensive gasoline, lubricants, replacement parts, tires, etc.

William Pawley was at the center of this important Mafia maneuver. He owned substantial interests in the old Havana Electric Railway. After liquidating the trolley system of Havana, he transferred its affairs to the so-called Compañía Cubana de Autobuses. A group of gangster elements of the Auténtico Party government, which controlled the labor union, was also implicated in these dealings.

The scandal that attended the dismantling of Havana's trolley system — people were made to believe that it was inefficient and not cost-efficient — roused much public opinion, "naturally silencing the turbulent negotiations in the operation between William Pawley and the high authorities, so scandalous that they prompted memorable debates in congress."[7] Washington's choice of Pawley was truly wise. He was a friend of Batista's. They had known each other for more than 20 years. Besides, Pawley was the owner, in 1958, of one of the most important municipal bus companies in the Cuban capital.

It has been possible to reconstruct that Pawley traveled to Havana in 1958, not just to propose to Batista that he quickly abandon the country, but also to form a new government capable of impeding the advance of the revolution, aided by the U.S. intelligence services. The idea was to use a group of top military officers tied to U.S. intelligence, and to certain figures in traditional politics who (in a calculated way) had kept a discreet distance from events.

The U.S. ambassador, Earl E. T. Smith, had already tried to persuade Batista to leave Cuba, but Smith had failed. Therefore, it was necessary for someone even more persuasive to intervene — someone considered by the Havana Mafia families (and especially Lansky) to be an effective intermediary between the economic groups, the Mafia and U.S. intelligence.

Some details of the secret mission undertaken by William D. Pawley were made known during a hearing held by a subcommittee of the Committee on the Judiciary of the U.S. Senate on September 2, 1960:

> Mr. Pawley: I was selected to go to Cuba to talk to Batista to see if I could convince him to capitulate, which I did. I spent three hours with him on the night of December 9.
>
> I was unsuccessful in my effort, but had Rubottom permitted me to say that "What I am offering you has tacit approval, sufficient governmental backing," I think Batista may have accepted it. I offered him an opportunity to live at Daytona Beach with his family, where his friends and family would not be molested; that we would make an effort to stop Fidel Castro from coming into power as a communist, but that the caretaker government would be men who were enemies of his, otherwise it would not work, because Fidel Castro would have to lay down his arms or otherwise admit he was a revolutionary fighting only because he wanted power, not because he was against Batista.
>
> Senator Keating: And the new government would also be unfriendly to Castro?
>
> Mr. Pawley: Yes.[8]

The supposed "difference" between the CIA and the State Department, especially in the last months of 1958, contributed to covering up the treacherous U.S. policy carried out against the Cuban nation. Washington controlled U.S. political policy toward Cuba during the years of Batista's dictatorship (1952-58) at the highest levels. To understand that long process, it is best to briefly examine an assessment made by Wise and Ross in their book, *The Invisible Government*, about the political policies implemented by the CIA and the State Department during the 1950s:

> In this, Foster Dulles reflected the U.S. ethic; the world as we would like it to be. While he took this public position, his brother was free to deal with nastier realities, to overturn governments and to engage in backstage political maneuvers all over the globe with the CIA's almost unlimited funds. He was, as Allen Dulles once put it, able to "fight fire with fire"

in a less than perfect world. Because he was equally dedicated in his own secret sphere, it was under Allen Dulles's stewardship that the CIA enjoyed its greatest expansion, particularly in the field of government-shaking secret operations overseas.

In pursuing this dual foreign policy, these special operations were largely kept secret from the U.S. people. The exception, of course, was when something went wrong, as at the Bay of Pigs.

This is not to say that the same two-sided foreign policy would never have evolved had the director of the CIA and the secretary of state not been brothers. It very likely would have. But the natural friction between the objectives and methods of the diplomats and the "spooks," between the State Department and the CIA, was to an extent reduced because of the close working relationship of the Dulles brothers. There was consequently less of a check and balance.

In a sense, one might say the Dulles brothers were predestined to take over the levers of power in the conduct of U.S. foreign affairs.[9]

While the "multiple" man, William D. Pawley, appeared in Havana to persuade Batista, the State Department retired its ambassador, Earl E. T. Smith, claiming he had to travel to Washington for consultation. But when it became evident that Batista would not accept even Pawley's proposal, Smith hastily returned, showing the "other face" of U.S. foreign policy: with the ultimatum that the general quit the country.

Certainly, beginning in November, the imperial forces (with the exception of the Havana-based Mafia families) had decided that the U.S. scheme of dominance over Cuba demanded, in addition to Batista's urgent departure, a series of covert operations aimed at preventing the Cuban people from attaining real power through revolution.

Batista's meeting with Ambassador Smith took place at the Finca Kuquine. Smith had requested it on December 14, through the Ministry of State of the dictatorship. But Batista, in a process that lasted three days, met with the U.S. ambassador on the night of December 17, a day after the Falcon Bridge in the central province of Las Villas was blown apart, leaving the island divided in half.

Smith was the bearer of Washington's official communiqué: Batista was to abandon the country immediately. Batista expressed his refusal again; not just to buy time, but to invoke the old scheme of domination imposed by the United States ever since the first third of the century. It is necessary to say that, in addition to the multiple operations mounted by U.S. intelligence in Cuba, U.S. intelligence agencies continued advising and supplying resources to the dictatorship.

The intelligence agencies were organizing various provocations aimed at creating a conflict of broad scope between the Rebel Army and the U.S. Government, which would permit Washington to legalize an intervention. These operations, organized by the CIA, were nothing new to Ambassador Smith. They were undertaken principally in the war zones, in the province of Oriente. They included the retreat of Batista's troops guarding the aqueduct of Yateras, which provided water to the U.S. naval base at Guantánamo, so the installations could be occupied by U.S. troops. Elite troops guarding the mining interests of the Rockefeller financial group were also told to retreat, so the columns of the Frank País Front could occupy the installations and villages near Nicaro. This move converted the zone into a theater of war, allowing brutal bombardments from Batista's airforce, which endangered the lives of U.S. citizens and their families. Even U.S. warships were mobilized, including the giant aircraft carrier *U.S.S. Franklin Delano Roosevelt,* which was stationed at that time a few miles from the Cuban coast. There were also conflicts with the U.S. naval base at Guantánamo, from which Batista's airforce was supplied for the constant bombardment of rural areas. For these operations, there was a precise coordination between Batista's government and the U.S. embassy in Havana. But these covert maneuvers failed time and again, thanks to the skill with which the rebel command confronted the growing hostility of the United States.

The U.S. ambassador, Earl E. T. Smith, was by no means a professional diplomat, but rather an influential broker on the New York Stock Exchange. He lived in Palm Beach and had important connections in Florida. It has been confirmed that Smith's presence in Cuba was not owing to his interest in representing the United States, but rather to his close ties with dominant financial groups in Cuba, especially those related to mining in Oriente Province.

Smith was an important stockholder in the Moa Bay Mining Company, charged with exploiting Cuban nickel deposits.[10] The financial groups feared that the revolutionary war in Cuba would affect their grand enterprises: at that time, they had US$75 million invested in Moa and US$100 million in Nicaro. Most importantly, there was a substantial operation going on between Batista and Washington; certain arrangements that permitted these financial groups to exploit the mines of Oriente and ship the minerals duty-free, which resulted in Cuba's losing almost US$40 million, according to the calculations of experts. Smith, of course, was tangled up in these dealings.

Ambassador Smith and General Batista met on the night of December 17, 1958. While this meeting took place, rebel forces directed by Fidel Castro and columns led by Raúl Castro and Juan Almeida prepared to tighten an iron circle around Santiago de Cuba. Che Guevara and Camilo Cienfuegos, meanwhile, had unleashed a large-scale offensive against the troops occupying principal cities linked by the central highway, from Santo Domingo to the limits of the province of Camagüey.

Smith wrote:

> After the usual diplomatic and pleasant exchanges of greetings, I asked [Foreign Minister Guell] for an appointment with the president. "It is my unpleasant duty," I said, "'to inform the president of the republic that the United States will no longer support the present government of Cuba and that my government believes that the president is losing effective control…"
>
> Although he paled at my statements he remained calm.[11]

Without wasting words, Smith conveyed Washington's decision to Batista, but it would come as no surprise to the general, who had already been informed by his multiple contacts. The dictator ignored Washington's ultimatum, so it must be assumed that Batista was under great pressure from the Mafia. For his part, the ambassador, surely knowing what was at stake, defined his participation in the following manner:

> In accordance with my instructions, I conveyed to the president that the State Department would view with skepticism any plan on his part, or any intention on his part, to remain in Cuba indefinitely. The president asked if he could come to Florida with his family to visit his home in Daytona

Beach. I suggested Batista spend a year or more in Spain or some other
foreign country and that he should not delay his departure from Cuba
beyond the time necessary for an orderly transition of power...

The United States had diplomatically, but clearly, told the president
of the republic that he should absent himself from his country.[12]

Batista resisted Washington's orders until the last minute, but
certainly not out of valor or conviction. Smith spoke of installing a
new transitional government that was the apparent enemy of Batista
and the true enemy of Fidel Castro. Batista, for his part, spoke of
constitutionality and of the supposed right of Rivero Agüero to assume
the presidency, as a result of the fraudulent elections of November,
1958. Without coming to an agreement with Smith, Batista at last
abandoned the Finca Kuquine around midnight.

Batista's resistance to a decision that Washington had taken during
the second half of November reveals the power of the Mafia families
who controlled the Havana empire. They were not simply a marginal
element, especially because of their links with important financial
groups, politicians in the United States and intelligence agents. Even
in the last days of 1958, the Havana-based Mafia hoped they might
still be able to manipulate events and create alternative options. Their
purpose was to stave off invasion by their traditional enemies: the
rest of the U.S. Mafia, with whom they had, one way or another, been
at war over the rights to Cuba, since 1956.

In the face of Batista's refusal (really, the refusal of Havana's
Mafia groups) the U.S. Government found itself in an extremely
embarrassing situation. It could not attack the Mafia, it could not take
Batista off the island, and least of all could it impede the advance of
the Rebel Army.

Consequently, as of December 17, 1958, Batista was definitively
abandoned by the United States. This explains the punishment he
subsequently received for having disobeyed Washington. From that
date, he was not allowed entry into the United States, access that had
been offered to him only a few days before; revealing the trickery of
the corrupt U.S. policy. After Batista's escape, just a few hours before
the Rebel Army began its advance toward Havana, he could not
even take refuge in Spain. The Mafia groups had to negotiate asylum

for Batista in the Dominican Republic, where they held substantial business interests and had old ties. (Detailed study of the period shows that the Dominican dictator Trujillo, from the 1940s, was allowed to use Havana as an intelligence center, to neutralize or smash activities and plans of the Dominican revolutionary movement.)

Although they had still not removed Batista from Cuba, the U.S. special services launched, in the last 10 to 12 days of 1958, a series of broad operations directed at paralyzing, diluting or neutralizing the advance of the revolution. These operations appeared to be inevitable and "natural" events, as the regime crumbled in the face of the revolutionary movement's offensive, but in reality were desperate operations mounted by U.S. intelligence.

1) The first operation was related to the efforts made by General Cantillo in the combat zone itself. Cantillo negotiated a meeting with the commander-in-chief of the Rebel Army and informed him of an anti-Batista plot in the ranks of the army of the dictatorship. The plan was very simple: to arrange for the revolution to take power along with the forces that, until that moment, had served the dictatorship.

How did Fidel Castro deal with this maneuver, orchestrated by U.S. intelligence? He did not respond with a flat refusal. It was necessary, as far as possible, to prevent useless bloodshed, and Castro agreed to the offer, so the civil war between Cubans might cease. Castro demanded, however, an essential condition. For any alliance with government troops at that moment opposed to Batista, elemental justice to the people demanded a key condition. In no case could the main culprits escape. Those who had dragged the Cuban nation through six years of crime, systematic robbery, excess and suffering would certainly have to face justice.

When General Cantillo returned to Havana and reported Castro's reply to the operational center of U.S. intelligence, it was no surprise that the rebel leader's conditions were not accepted. Cantillo, therefore, did not return to Oriente, and the operation was considered finished.

2) The second maneuver mounted by U.S. intelligence revolved around Batista's departure. This was in the early morning of January 1, 1959. It involved a typical coup d'état, using the oldest magistrate

in Cuba as president and Cantillo himself as chief of the armed forces. By then, U.S. intelligence had lost all initiative (which it would not recover.) The manipulations of the revolution of 1930 were a thing of the past. Now, a whole people had rallied around a determined leader, in support of an armed, battle-tested Rebel Army.

How did Fidel Castro react to this second operation? He spoke to the whole population by means of Radio Rebelde, inciting a general popular revolutionary strike from the combat zone itself, while the Rebel Army continued military operations against enemy positions and armed resistance to the revolution.

3) In a desperate attempt, the CIA tried to place Colonel Barquín (imprisoned on the Isla de Pinos) as chief of staff of the military Camp Columbia, so he could contain the revolutionary movement. Barquín had supposedly won prestige by rebelling against Batista in the early months of 1956. He had been the naval, air force and military attaché of General Batista in Washington, and was a representative before the Inter-American Defense Council. In the early months of 1956, Barquín organized a conspiracy that was uncovered; and his fellow conspirators were arrested and jailed, until the triumph of the revolution. Barquín succeeded in rallying a small, if disparate, group of military officers. It is necessary to underscore that at the time, the Batista regime did not face any special problems or difficulties. There was no serious friction with the financial groups, with the Mafia families settled in Havana, with the U.S. intelligence community or with the Washington government, in particular with the Dulles brothers, whose interests were being wonderfully attended.

At that time, the Dulles brothers were about to compromise themselves with a destabilizing adventure against Batista.

When the Cuban Revolution placed imperialist rule in crisis, however, the director of the CIA personally suggested to President Eisenhower that drastic action be taken to avoid Fidel Castro's taking power. In addition to urgently removing Batista from Cuba, it was necessary to install a civil and military junta, as a transitional or emergency government, and the man proposed by Allen Dulles to head this complex operation was Colonel Barquín.

In the last days of December, 1959, U.S. intelligence also thought of placing Barquín in the Leoncio Vidal Regiment in Santa Clara, so he and Colonel Pedraza could take charge of the situation in the province and resist the forces commanded by Che Guevara. A helicopter was ready on the runway at the Columbia base to transfer Barquín from Isla de Pinos to the province of Santa Clara. However, at the last hour, in the face Che Guevara's uncontainable advance, that option was discarded, and it was decided that Barquín would try to resist or plot his way out defeat, from Camp Columbia.

No study has yet been undertaken to fully evaluate the complex and varied operations of the U.S. intelligence community in Cuba in 1958. (One such operation was the Menoyo option. The intelligence agents of the CIA and the Pentagon installed an operational center in the central region of Cuba, using the Segundo Frente Nacional del Escambray, with the purpose of supporting Eloy Gutiérrez Menoyo in opposition to the Cuban revolutionary movement.)[13]

So numerous and diverse were the parties involved at the time, any such study of U.S. intelligence operations would have to include people as unlikely as Errol Flynn. The actor apparently talked of launching an attack at night, as he drifted drunk through the brothels of Manzanillo after a vain attempt to climb the mountains of the Sierra Maestra. This and other operations came up later in the story of the treason of Sorí Marín, Miró Cardona (Grau's defense lawyer in the case of his robbery of US$74 million), Díaz Lanz and Huber Matos.

As the curtain was coming down on an era, certain people began to close their accounts in dazzling Havana, in spite of the fact that the Night and Day club was still capable of making its clients rich.

Drugs and gambling caused increasing delirium, along with the roulette wheels and card tables. The Rainbow, on the right bank of the Canimar River, maintained its excellent casino, bar, restaurant and a salon for shows. It was on the road to the beach at Varadero, between pleasure and good fortune, where memories still lingered of the stellar performances of Kary Russi and Susan Love, while Pepito Garcés directed the orchestra and marvelous Ñico Gelpi handled the productions.

Liberace's presence was again anticipated. He would arrive this time accompanied by his brother George and the Cuban Rogelio Darías, a favorite of the time, who had introduced percussion rhythms into the virtuoso's performances.

Xiomara Alfaro, Lucho Gatica, René Cabell, Olga Guillot and Celia Cruz occupied the spaces left by the foreign stars. Meanwhile, in every neighborhood in Havana, Victrola juke boxes poured out songs about abandonment, treachery and desperation, in a climate where the melodies of the extraordinary Beny Moré were incomparable.

The revolutionary movement in Havana organized a show with television artists, to be performed on January 1, in the Castillo del Príncipe, to celebrate the escape of political prisoners condemned to death.

On December 29 the airplane of Tony de Varona,[14] ex-senator and the former prime minister of Carlos Prío, landed at the airport at Santa Lucía in the north part of Camagüey, accompanied by two U.S. citizens. The airport had been constructed by elements tied to the Mafia. They also built a motel near the region's fine beaches. Varona had planned to land south of Camagüey, having agreed to bring in a shipment of arms. He actually landed in the extreme north of the province, assuming that with the imminent defeat of Batista's dictatorship, rebel troops that had risen up months ago would form part of the phantom group Organización Auténtica, and allow him to enter the city of Camagüey and demand political power.

It was too late for such schemes. The whole country was already in a state of insurrection and jubilation. The streets, parks and avenues of the capital overflowed with people. Crowds took over the city and began to smash the parking meters and gambling salons. They overturned card tables and roulette wheels. Slot machines were thrown into the street, and the people surrounded the regime's military defenses. Meanwhile, the guerrilla forces occupied Santiago de Cuba, and the columns of Camilo Cienfuegos and Che Guevara advanced toward Havana. It was a great stampede, and many couldn't leave fast enough. Thomas Duffin, John Jenkins, Irving Levitts, Mike Dade, Milton Warshaw, Robert E. Wytzel, Carl Layman, San Grace, Jack Walter Malone, Morris Segal, Duque Nolan and Frank

Curtis rapidly gathered their suitcases and appeared at the airport at Boyeros with their U.S. passports in hand, desperate to leave on the first plane out.

The Armando Feo affair was even wilder. Feo thought that everyone would forget his dealings with the great Lucky Luciano and that his presence in the principal casinos of the capital would be of no importance. Along with several friends, he occupied a police station and assigned himself the rank of *comandante*.

It was all part of a great last effort on the part of the U.S. Government to keep its power mechanisms intact in Cuba, but the Rebel Army had placed the scheme of imperial domination in total crisis.

The only move left for the U.S. financial-Mafia-intelligence groups was to begin immediately making secret demands, so the rulers in Washington might, at any cost and by whatever means, try to recuperate the splendid empire they had lost in Havana.

Appendix One:

The Luxury Hotels of Havana

It is necessary to emphasize that, at the beginning of 1950, Havana did not have a hotel infrastructure as it would have six or seven years later. By then, in addition to the wonderful Hotel Nacional, there was the Hotel Sevilla Biltmore and hotels such as the Presidente, Lincoln, Inglaterra, Royal Palm, and Plaza and others near the Parque Central in downtown Havana.

At first, the principal hotel capacity fell to apartment buildings of three or four floors, or apartment houses in the areas of Vedado or Miramar. There were villas or small motels devoted to international tourism, rented with all the amenities, including cooks and domestic servants. The building on the corner of 8th and 19th streets was one of these typical hotels, as were some others that proliferated on Third Street or in the vicinity of Havana's Malecón.

But with the reordering instigated by Batista's return to power, the construction of a further reaching infrastructure (grand, luxury hotels) was initiated, designed to transform Havana into a place of enjoyment for moneyed tourists from the United States.

The Cuban state assumed the most substantial investments in this hotel infrastructure; and in scarcely four years, a group of important hotels sprang up, notably the Hotel Internacional in Varadero, which prefigured this great hotel-building project.

By 1952, 29 hotels operated in Havana, with 3,118 rooms. Not all of them could accommodate upscale international tourism. When the specialists of the Mafia-special services considered the criminal state in Cuba had sufficiently stabilized, construction immediately began on a group of hotels considered first-rate: Vedado, St. John's, Comodoro, Colina, Lido, Rosita de Hornedo, Caribbean, Siboney, Habana Deauville,

Capri, Havana Hilton, Riviera and others. These Havana hotels elevated the capacity to 5,438 rooms, especially boosted by this last group, which belonged to the highest category of hotels in the world.

There were also other installations controlled by the Mafia in Varadero, in the duty-free zone of Isla de Pinos, in the mountainous region of Pinar del Río, in the accelerated project of Monte Carlo de La Habana and the modern motel Jagua in Cienfuegos.

To assume the construction and operation of this hotel chain (offering great casinos, drugs and sex) the Mafia utilized a group of front companies, private banks or other institutions created for the purpose.

The construction of the Hotel Capri on the corner of N and 21st (one of the exclusive areas of Vedado) was undertaken by means of a company run by Jaime Canavés. The ties between Canavés and the Mafia were very old. They had recourse to a company called Compañía Hotelera de La Habana so that, by means of BANDES, and with the intervention of José Manuel Martínez Zaldo, vice-president of the Banco Financiero, the Cuban State assumed the financing of the Capri in mid-1957.[1]

The Compañía Hotelera de La Habana had been constituted by Public Deed No. 1043, on December 12, 1956, by Jaime Canavés Lull, José Canavés Ugalde, Jaime Canavés Ugalde, Francisco de la Horra Diez and Dr. Mario Augusto Soto Román, having as its objective "to construct, purchase, operate, lease, and sublease buildings for hotels or for any other legitimate commercial business, with an authorized capital of $2 million."[2]

Jaime Canavés Lull was a Cuban citizen of Spanish origin, 73 years old, married to Felipa Petra Ugalde Sanz, a contractor and resident of Vedado. He had lived in Cuba since 1913, and earlier he had directed the Compañía Constructora Canavés.[3]

The Compañía Hotelera de La Habana began construction of the Hotel Capri, with the intention of inaugurating it in November 1957, with 241 rooms. Adjacent to the hotel would be a two-story building designed to house a grand casino and a nightclub that, according to the documentation, had been contracted by the Compañía Hotelera Shepard of Miami Beach, represented by Julius Shepard and Jack Lieberbaum. The latter were the president and vice-president of the Shepard Hotel Company, the people who (following the usual pattern), would lease the hotel after it was finished. In this case, it was for US$193,000 per year for the first three years, and thereafter for US$190,000 per year until the 20 years of the contract had been completed.[4]

A simple analysis of this transaction reveals that it amounted to a bald-faced mockery of the Cuban state. In summary, the said contract remained fixed at US$201,000 per year without any kind of credit.

The Compañía Jaime Canavés had been in existence since 1949, and The Trust Company of Cuba was the entity that offered it credits in the low six figures because of its "magnificent experience."

Julius Shepard and Jack Lieberbaum, for their part, operated the Hotel Leamington in Florida and had excellent references from the Mercantile National Bank of Miami.[5]

These recommendations were not only personal, but they extended also to the operations undertaken by the Compañía Hotelera Shepard. Furthermore, there were guarantees offered by the First National Bank.

In Cuba, the institution that provided cover for this operation was the Banco Financiero. Behind it was the law firm of Lendian y Lendian, with its offices on the corner of 21st and O, in charge of providing information and guarantees to BANDES.[6]

In a letter sent by the law firm of Lendian y Lendian, it is observed that both Mr. Shepard and Mr. Lieberbaum possess "hotel experience, Mr. Shepard having served for some time as administrator of the Hotel Leamington [notice how important these "visible heads" are][7] and Mr. Lieberbaum having served as the owner of hotels in Miami, currently serving as owner of the famous Dunes Motel on said beach."[8]

It is interesting to observe how the lawyer Armando Lendian (of the firm of Lendian y Lendian) based in the Sinclair building, was the secretary of the Compañía Hotelera Shepard, of which company Shepard was president and Lieberbaum vice-president.

As part of all these schemes, it is fascinating to read a note written by Ectore Reynaldo, assistant manager and chief of credit and securities of BANDES, about the Hotel Capri: "Our intervention would be to make the Banco Financiero [Lobo's bank][9] competitive and to take away business from the bank that already has it and that we deem can undertake the financing without our intervention."[10]

It is a well-known fact of international history that, after its inauguration, the Hotel Capri was run by the actor George Raft, during his memorable gangster days in Havana.

In the case of the Hotel Havana Hilton, funds from the Caja del Retiro y Asistencia Social de los Trabajadores Gastronómicos were used for the project.[11] Besides the "directors" of the Sindicato Gastronómico, institutions created in the 1950s were also part of this operation.

The Sindicato labor union "leaders" had fulfilled their terms of office. However, on May 6, 1957, General Batista issued a certain resolution 12 to prolong until January 1959 the terms of delegates making up the Board of Directors of the Caja del Retiro y Asistencia Social de los Trabajadores Gastronómicos, so that they could make arrangements with the front company. Batista, Prime Minister Andrés Rivero Agüero and Minister of Labor José Suárez Rivas (brother of Eduardo Suárez Rivas) signed the resolution. Agüero, of course, was the man with whom the Mafia groups aspired to continue the criminal state toward the end of 1958.

For the front company maneuver, Batista used Efren Jesús Pertierra Linero (Pertierra again), Francisco Aguirre and Andrés Castellano Martínez. Representatives of BANDES and Francisco Miguel Acosta Rendueles, the director of the Banco de Comercio Exterior, were present at a meeting held to sign the document (outlining the arrangement), during which the resources for the hotel investments were submitted.

At the beginning, the investment for the Hotel Havana Hilton was US$14 million; but the costs later rose to US$21,793,548.[13] The project was undertaken by the U.S. firm Welton Becket Associates of Los Angeles, California, and BANDES assumed the remainder of the investment, for the amount of US$13.5 million, under the charge of the BNC.

For its part, the Sindicato Gastronómico invested more that US$6 million in the Hotel Havana Hilton. When it was completed, however, the hotel did not fall under the operation of that labor union, nor did it go to any Cuban company, but to a U.S. one.

The document that legalized this operation established that the investment assumed by BANDES was made with an interest rate of 4.5 percent (soft credit) payable through the Banco de Comercio Exterior de Cuba. Much earlier, however, on November 24, 1953, a lease had been agreed with the Hilton Hotel International for 1.3 million pesos annually, just a little less than 150,000 pesos of the total amount of interest payable in a year.

It was a solid deal, entirely legal. The Mafia took charge of setting up a grand casino, along with other interests representing millions of dollars. In July 1958 (to cite just one example) the payroll of the Casino of the Hotel Havana Hilton included a list of more than 20 U.S. *mafiosi* who paid Social Security in Cuba.[14] They were: Harry Miller, David Geiger, Larry Sonfsky, Joe and Charles Sileci, Sal A. Parisey, Allen Kanter, Vincent Brennan, Velma Garfinkle, Emanuel Charfer, Joe Lo Pinto, George Frentress, George Labandie, Jimmy Morrow, John Bandik, Donte Carmesino, Luis J. Ross, Samuel Gremblatt, Jack Moore, George McAroy, James Baker, Vern Stone, Luis Garfinkle, John Achuff, Patrick Smith and Robert Ryne.

The opening of the Hotel Deauville, situated on Galiano Street, between San Lázaro and the Malecón, was characteristic of the period of construction of luxury hotels-casinos operated by the Mafia.

We have used archival documents to examine the other hotels, but will discuss the Hotel Deauville by means of a series of statements by former food workers, gathered by Benigno Iglesias Trabadelo, a food worker and direct witness of these operations.

Benigno wrote an (unpublished) book entitled *El primero de enero y el Hotel Deauville* based on his own personal experiences and those of work colleagues.[15] The latter included: Lorenzo Sosa Martínez, Humberto Fernández, Rafael Carballido, Bruno Rodríguez, Juan Rivera, Emilio Martínez Hernández (whose last name was Prieto and ran the corner grocery store) and others who knew many details.[16]

The Hotel Deauville began construction in 1956 on land belonging to Agustín Tamargo, then a journalist with *Bohemia* magazine. The project was also overseen by a front company, and rapidly began to be run by Mafia elements, among them Saint Kay, Mr. Ross, Mr. Maylo, Evaristo Rodríguez Fernández ("visible head" in the luxury casino) and a man of Italian origin naturalized in the United States known as Martini. There was also the occasional presence of George Raft and the permanent control of Santo Trafficante Jr.

The Deauville had 140 rooms, a pool and cabañas, spacious and luxurious gambling salons, a bar next to a theater for pornographic shows and a small restaurant. It also had a popular casino in the basement, with an entrance on San Lázaro Street isolated from the rest of the hotel.

Like almost all of the Mafia's hotels in Havana, the Deauville's principal business was not leasing rooms. The rooms remained reserved for particular guests or visitors who arrived by boat or plane. The Deauville offered its visitors (or invited guests) rooms, meals, drugs and women (especially pornographic shows) all absolutely free. The premise was that the guests, inebriated by the tropical charm, beautiful women and the delirious flow of drugs, would then enter the gambling salons. Or, if they preferred, they were offered small salons for more intimate parties.

Room 222 had sophisticated installations, employing techniques such as special cameras and equipment to monitor the results and players and to observe dealers in the casino gaming rooms.

Witnesses confirm that Meyer Lansky, Walter Clark, Marquin Kraus, Lety Clark, Roman Normain, Frank Sinatra and other famous people attended the hotel's inauguration.

What is certain is that Santo Trafficante Jr. was always in direct control of the Deauville (he also ran the Sans Souci cabaret) and that the hotel's inauguration was attended by "an army of bouncers who protected these gentlemen."[17] Benigno offers this account of the days when the Havana groups were taking their battle to U.S. territory:

> In those days, furthermore, people were arriving in our country who were tainted by villainous and criminal activities, mixed up in the assassination of the gangster Anastasia. They had taken Cuba for the headquarters of their villainy…[18] They employed drink subtly with drugs, in plain view of everyone, and later proceeded to gambling, and finally pornography, and concluded with the classic private bacchanalia.[19]

The Mafia, of course, tried to give the hotel a respectable atmosphere: gentlemen in tuxedos, and ladies that pretended to move in a great bourgeois ambience, while the closed-circuit cameras and special vigilance watched and controlled everything.

Finally, in several rooms of the Hotel Deauville equipment had been installed for the filming of pornographic movies destined for the foreign market. According to witnesses, it was common to use young women, with those conducting the trade often employing force, or deceiving the women with false promises.[20]

The Hotel Havana Riviera, on the corner of Malecón and Paseo, was known internationally as the flagship hotel of the "financier of the Mafia." As Frederic Sondern Jr. tells us:

> Meyer Lansky, the big New York gambler, and a group of his friends had the necessary money and saw the financial possibilities. Meyer himself acquired the

concession in the magnificent new US$14 million Riviera Hotel on the Malecón; his brother, Jack, established more decorous but equally profitable gaming rooms in the older but opulent Hotel Nacional. Other tourist centers were assigned to a group of carefully selected casino executives.[21]

These were part of the new alliances that Lansky had made, beginning in 1956, against the efforts of the Mafia families of New York, who demanded participation in the lucrative business affairs in Havana.[22]

As part of that expansion in the 1950s, Lansky created the typical front company, Compañía Hotelera La Riviera de Cuba, to take charge of construction and operation of a future hotel chain in Havana, besides attending to the Hotel Riviera itself.

The Compañía Hotelera La Riviera de Cuba, consisted in an official (and legal) manner of the following people: Harry Smith, Julies E. Rosengard, Benjamin Seigel, Irving Feldman, Edward Levinson, Eduardo Suárez Rivas and Juan Francisco López García.

To legalize the construction of the Hotel Riviera, a meeting was held attended by Canadian citizen Harry Smith (the same man who ran the Jockey Club in Havana in 1942) as president of the company; Juan Ramón Rodríguez Rivera, assistant general manager of BANDES; and "José Manuel Martínez Zaldo, native of New York, Cuban citizen, of legal age, married, banker and resident of this city on San Ignacio Street No. 104, who attended the meeting representing Lobo's Banco Financiero."[23, 24]

The Hotel Riviera was conceived at a cost of US$11 million (the Cuban State assumed an investment of more than US$8 million) but the cost grew to US$14 million. The hotel had:

> ...21 floors, with 378 rooms, dining rooms, casino, cabaret, cabaña club, swimming pool, park, gardens, other luxurious salons for public use, 2,600 square meters of commercial area and other specifications that make up the project, plans and descriptive memoranda prepared by the firm, Feldman Construction Company, of Miami Beach, Florida, United States of America, authorized in Cuba by the architect Manuel Carrera Machado.[25]

The relevant document for the Riviera transaction was signed (before the notary public Augusto Maxwell de la Coba) by Smith; J. R. Rod; José Manuel Martínez Zaldo, the "financier" and E. León Soto representing BANDES. In attached documents, the well-known Eduardo Suárez Rivas also appears, in his capacity as secretary of the Compañía de Hoteles La Riviera de Cuba.

These documents observe that the Hotel Riviera had been projected: "to house in the luxury hotels themselves places of entertainment or casinos to operate games of chance, authorized by the so-called Law of Tourism and other legislation that prevails in Cuba."[26]

The established ties of the U.S. Mafia to the Banco Financiero were maintained in an unaltered manner until after 1958, until the beginning of the process of recuperation of the riches that belonged to the Cuban nation. Proof of this fidelity is the letter sent by Dr. Eladio Ramírez, then vice-president of the Banco Financiero, dated July 6, 1959, addressed to Dr. Felipe Pazos, who then presided over the BNC. Let us look at these passages:

> We want to take advantage of this opportunity to tell you that our bank has handled the account of the Hotel Riviera from the beginning, and we can make the following affirmations in a completely responsible manner:[27]

> 1) That the investment by the stockholders in the amount of US$5,580,000 is registered with us, and we have handled the corresponding funds. We have all the data and antecedents in our possession and we place them at your disposition.

> 2) That the accounting for the company during the period of the execution of the works was audited by the Department of Inspection (public accountants) and engineers of the Technical Department of BANDES.

> 3) Likewise, BANDES always had an architect at the building site who supervised and checked the construction, without whose report no bill was paid.

> 4) That the man who, from the beginning of the negotiations, in his capacity as treasurer of the company, and who was in contact with us and who continues still to direct the hotel, is a lawyer from Boston, Dr. Julies E. Rosengard, who is at the same time public accountant, a man with a personal fortune, about whom we had the best reports from the Royal Bank of Canada, the First National City Bank of New York and the Chemical and Corn Exchange Bank of New York, copies of which we send you. We know his wife, also, who belongs to a distinguished and wealthy family from Boston, a person of great culture and refinement; we also know his two children, and we can assure you that they are people of exquisite demeanor and of impeccable habits. Mr. Rosengard is a member of the Board of Trustees of the University of Suffolk in Boston, Massachusetts.

> 5) We know also the first president of the company, Harry Smith, who with his brothers operates the Hotel Prince George, one of the best in Toronto, Canada. They have vast investments in mining companies. We are enclosing the banking references that we obtained from these gentlemen.

> 6) Likewise, we know firsthand Irving Feldman of Miami, where he is favorably known as a contractor and an honorable person, having constructed a multitude of works of great scope all over the United States, and who was the one who personally directed the construction of the hotel, during which he demonstrated extraordinary ability and experience, meeting the challenge in terms of time, quality, and efficiency. He is the current president of the company because of the resignation of Harry Smith.[28]

> 7) We enclose the list of stockholders. For the majority we have few references, a result of not having had any relations or contact with them; but nobody has told us that they have antecedents that could render embarrassing their moral conduct.

> These men have made an enormous investment in our country. They observe our laws, they respect our customs, and if we truly want to stimulate investments in

Cuba, we have to guarantee them the capital that is already invested and which is creating jobs and sources of wealth.

8) There has been much speculation about the moral conduct of the new hotel keepers; but lamentably we have confused the clean, honest, and respectable business of the hotels with that of the casinos, which unfortunately in many cases has been handled by people who do not come preceded by good references. We are undertaking the healthy task of cleaning up this situation, a task that is very well received by public opinion in general and by the hotel keepers themselves, who instead of resenting this clean up, cooperate sincerely and enthusiastically in this effort to purify our public customs in a sector as difficult as the houses and centers of games of chance.

9) In summary: the persons who comprise the company that operates the Hotel Riviera have made in Cuba, under the shelter of our laws, a considerable investment of money, they have constructed a hotel that is the pride of Cuba and which can compare favorably to the best hotels of its class all over the world. They have no unfavorable references regarding the origin of the invested money, nor in terms of their moral conduct. They have operated their business, from its origin in 1956 until now, respecting the laws and customs, employing carefully selected Cuban personnel in both the construction of the building and in the operation of the hotel. The crisis through which the hotel is passing is due only and exclusively to external factors out of their control. In the winter season 1957-58, they had reasonable profits, although they were quite inferior to the million pesos that have been absorbed, together with the labor capital on which they counted, because of the unfortunate circumstances that have prevailed in Cuban during the whole year of 1958 and the first months of the current year of 1959. Fortunately, this has been overcome partly, which allows them to look to the future with confidence. But if these unjust and unfounded *prejudices* are maintained against the men who made the initial investment and there is not an effective cooperation to make the business cost-effective,[29] reducing the artificial and hyper-inflated payroll that currently prevails, the business is condemned to rotund failure, and from now on we tell you that it is not worthwhile to invest healthy money, that it is too little and too late and that the inevitable collapse of the company cannot be avoided, which will result inexorably in prejudicing the country and in discouraging all possibilities of new investments, without which our second sugar crop, tourism, will be impossible.[30]

Appendix Two:

The Banco Financiero and the Cuban Sugar Industry

On July 11, 1952, Dr. Joaquín Martínez Sáenz (president of the Banco Nacional de Cuba) received a communication soliciting authorization for the opening of the Banco de La Habana.[1] This bank would have its first branch in the town of Niquero in the province of Oriente, where the sugar mills Niquero, Media Luna and Cabo Cruz were located. The Campechuela, San Ramón and Santa Rita sugar mills and other agricultural and commercial businesses were also in this area, but there was no banking entity. According to the proposal put to the BNC, the bank would be national in character and have its central office at San Ignacio Street Nos. 104-108, in Havana.[2]

The persons interested in opening the bank were the following:

Julio Lobo Olavarría, stockholder and director of the parent companies of the Tinguaro, Escambray, Niquero, Cabo Cruz, Caracas and other sugar mills. (Lobo also directed the international commercial entity, Galbán Trading Company and a number of related companies.)

Germán S. López Sánchez, who was stockholder and director of the parent companies of the Santa María, El Pilar, Caracas, Najasa and Siboney sugar mills. Sánchez was also a member of the Banco Cacicedo of Cienfuegos and associated with commercial and port enterprises in that city.

Gregory Escogedo Salmón, stockholder and director of the Fidencia, Perseverancia, El Pilar, Caracas, Najasa and Siboney sugar mills, and of livestock and rice companies.

Dr. Eladio Ramírez León, ex-president of the Asociación de Hacendados de Cuba, lawyer, director and stockholder in the Tánamo and Unión sugar mill companies.

Ignacio Carvajal Olivares, stockholder and director of the La Francia and San Cristóbal sugar mills, and member of the company Carvajal (wholesale grocers);

president and stockholder of the Banco Carvajal of Artemisa and a member of other commercial enterprises.

Simeón Ferro Martínez, stockholder and director of the parent companies of the San Cristóbal and La Francia sugar mills, member of the commercial firm Hijo de Pío Ferro and the company Industrial Ferro, and a member of other commercial enterprises.

Dr. Fernando de la Riva Domínguez, lawyer and stockholder in the Covadonga and Constancia sugar mills.

George Fowler y Suárez del Villar, stockholder and president of the North American Sugar Company, parent company of the Narcisa sugar mill.

José García Palomino, stockholder and director of the Galbán Trading Company. Also Enrique Sotto León, lawyer and professor of Economics at the Escuela Profesional de Comercio de La Habana. These two men were secretary and director, respectively, of the parent companies of the Perseverancia and Tánamo sugar mills.

The majority of these people were lesser stockholders and "visible heads" of businesses within Lobo's orbit. The Banco de La Habana was constituted with the authorization of US$2 million but it initially began to operate with a capital of only US$200,000. On July 18, 1952, the project was reordered. The Banco de La Habana was converted into the Banco Financiero. By September 16 of that year, L. Rangel, vice-president of The Trust Company of Cuba, informed the BNC that the Banco Financiero had proceeded to open in the BNC an account for the sum of US$260,000.

At the beginning of October 1952, Lobo designated Francisco M. Acosta y Rendueles as administrator of the Banco Financiero. Rendueles had 30 years of banking experience in the offices of the National City Bank of Havana. It was not until October 21, however, that the Banco Financiero deposited in the Trust Company of Cuba a check for US$100,000, as a centralized reserve to begin its operations.

The initial operations of the Banco Financiero were directed toward a group of sugar mills that Lobo controlled or would later control. In general, they formed part of a sugar empire based on commercial dealings in raw sugar, which had its offices in several cities in the United States, Puerto Rico and important European capitals.

Of Lobo it was said that he became the heir to old, established businesses. In the Telephone Directory of 1937,[3] there appears an advertisement for Galbán Lobo y Compañía, importers and exporters since 1864, and now with branches for sugar, drugs, chemical products, lubricants, rubber, hardware, wholesale groceries, honey, wax and vegetables. There were also departments for fire, automobile and maritime transportation insurance.

To date, there has been no study of the origins of Julio Lobo's fortunes or of his ties and real dimensions. Lobo enjoyed all prerogatives in Cuba. He was seen as a very important Cuban industrial and financial leader, although his true nationality was not even clear. It is said that he was of Jewish origin and that his real name was Julius Wolf, born in Holland, Aruba or Venezuela. Some of his old collaborators affirm that, with the advent of the Great Depression of 1929, and at the beginning of the 1930s, he went broke and was on the verge of ruin. By the decade of the 1940s, however, his fortune was already considerable. Numerous references in the press of the day attest that Lobo was becoming wealthy out of black market ventures and by speculating on products that became essential for World War II. Later he profited from the fraudulent schemes of the Auténtico Party.

In the second half of the 1940s, Lobo was the victim of an attack, when Auténtico Party gangsters, who demanded that he hand over a large sum, accused him of being an important speculator. In reality, not a few of Lobo's economic resources came from his earnings as a speculator. What is not explainable historically is how, in the midst of the great imperialist forces that disputed the economic dominion of Cuba, and especially the interests of the coveted sugar industry, Lobo succeeded in controlling a great empire based on the production and commercialization of raw Cuban sugar. The vertiginous expansion of his business affairs was amazing.

Documents regarding Lobo's success remain in the archives, of course, but are usually manipulated to cover up the most revealing data. In any case, the evidence demonstrates that, by at least 1954, the interests of the U.S. Mafia began to operate in a direct manner in the Banco Financiero.

Once considered a marginal group in Cuban society, the U.S. Mafia's operations have not been given the attention they deserve. What is now undeniable, however, is that the business affairs of the Mafia in Cuba included not only casinos and hotels, high-class prostitution and drug channels, but also other less visible interests, which were handled so as not to leave a trace. The petty legalistic machinery of contemporary capitalism protected these lesser interests. The Mafia's affairs in Cuba included increasingly more profitable sectors of the Cuban economy, international connections of great magnitude, socio-cultural connections and meddling in Cuban politics.

In the case of sugar, there is yet to be a study of the transformation that occurred as part of the maneuvers of 1937-38, in which General Batista appeared as the craftsman of the Ley de Coordinación Azucarera y Moratoria Hipotecaria (Law of Sugar Coordination and Mortgage Moratorium). Due to special circumstances, including international events of the time, there began a 15-year period in which radical changes took place, reflected in statistics concerning the owners of a considerable number of sugar mills. This change would give rise to many theories, some of them increasingly less believable. Among the latter were those claiming the Cuban sugar industry was no longer profitable. According to this view, it had reached a point of absolute saturation and the powerful U.S. companies had lost interest in this sector. It was as though Cuban sugar did not offer the imperialist system of exploitation four fabulous channels of wealth, of which only two have been studied halfway.

The profitability of the sugar industry in Cuba was always guaranteed by ferocious exploitation: the hunger, unemployment, sweat and blood of Cuban workers.

The four great channels of imperial wealth of the Cuban sugar industry were the following: 1) Profits obtained by the companies themselves, or by the owners or stockholders of the sugar mills. 2) The hundreds of millions of dollars that each year fed the coffers of the U.S. state, from tariffs levied on Cuban sugar so it could enter the United States. From 1921 to 1929, from this source alone, US$1,119 million flowed into the U.S. budget. This represented 37 percent of the total value of the sugar exported. 3) The lucrative interest received by the banking system (international financial center located in Havana) from financing the sugar crop. Everything seems to indicate that this was the new method of exploiting the Cuban sugar industry. In this manner, substantial dividends were obtained, which passed directly over to U.S. financial capital. 4) The abundant earnings produced by the commercialization of this sugar, increasingly dominated by a monopoly.

To explain this magical act, by means of which the sugar industry began to "pass" into the hands of Cuban capital (not a few times into the hands of the elements that made up the political-military leadership) one would doubtlessly have to consider other factors.

What is certain is that, before the U.S. Mafia began to operate in this overt manner in the Banco Financiero, the bank confronted a precarious situation, if not a total stagnation, in spite of the multiple operations it was handling with the sugar mills. Banking losses had even been reported; and, a few months later, ridiculous earnings. This increase was owing to the fact that the Galbán Trading Company was manipulating checks for foreign deals and effecting currency exchanges.

By that stage, the crisis of the Banco Financiero was such that the BNC did not approve its proposed line of credit for the group of sugar mills that were in Lobo's orbit. The BNC alleged that the Banco Financiero did not have sufficient deposits, and the credits were destined for sugar mills that were tied to the entity by means of stockholders and directors. By then Dr. Joaquín Martínez Sáenz (president of the BNC) was urging the 70 banks in the system to acquire public works debt certificates.

At the meeting of directors of the Banco Financiero, it was agreed that the administrator Acosta Rendueles would approach Martínez Sáenz to accept the judicial order. The intermediary for these arrangements was Víctor Pedroso, president of the Asociación de Bancos de Cuba and vice-president and administrator of the Banco Pedroso.

Similarly, as part of the pressure on the Banco Financiero, a "message" was sent to Lobo: the BNC could retract the authorization to accept reserve accounts, which would be available only to the banks that participated in "the signing and floating of the state's securities; this list would be updated periodically."[4]

The certificates the BNC wanted to finance had been issued for the construction of the Palace of Justice and the Ministry of Communications. The Banco Financiero was also told that a positive response in the matter would enable them to accept accounts of the Instituto Cubano de Estabilización del Azúcar [Cuban Institute for the Stabilization of Sugar]. They might also be able to accept future accounts of the Caja del Retiro Azucarero [Savings Fund for the Retirement of Sugar Workers] and other official organisms connected with the government.

At the beginning of 1954, Lobo disappeared from Havana. It was affirmed, however, that he was making a pleasure trip to New York, (a trip that was strangely out of keeping with Lobo's usual habits.) His private secretary, Carlota Steegers Plasencia, would attend to his affairs in Lobo's absence. His absence was then prolonged for several months; more significantly, his return coincided with the entrance into his bank of important elements of the Mafia families ruled by Amadeo Barletta Barletta, in the persons of José Manuel Martínez Zaldo, José Guash and Amadeo himself, among others.

Furthermore, while Lobo was away, Francisco M. Acosta Rendueles was authorized to occupy the position of trustee,[5] on any commission for bonds or mortgage promissory notes "in the manner and under the conditions that the board authorizes… without any limitation."[6]

It was precisely during the time of Julio Lobo's trip that great changes took place at the Banco Financiero. The veteran vice-president resigned and was replaced by José Manuel Martínez Zaldo, one of the key men in the Mafia operations of the Barletta family.

The changes within the Banco Financiero also coincided with General Batista's designation (by means of the president of the BNC) of Francisco Acosta Rendueles as director of the recently created Banco de Comercio Exterior de Cuba.

These matters were handled with such duplicity that in the relevant Banco Financiero proceedings, Lobo appears profoundly offended by Rendueles, subjecting him to insults and biting invective and almost unleashing a small war of words. Could it be that Lobo looked unfavorably upon one of his men being chosen to direct the Banco de Comercio Exterior de Cuba, from which Lobo could make (and did make) such good business deals? Such was the feigning that, in one of the Banco Financiero's records,[7] Lobo appears to deny his veteran administrator his most fundamental rights, declaring himself, before the bank's board of directors and the rest of the stockholders, as the sworn enemy of Rendueles. Was Lobo really such a clumsy man?

The directors were without a doubt too powerful for Batista to easily confer such a distinction upon Acosta Rendueles; and Lobo's "protests" were not convincing.

During the meeting in question,[8] it was also announced that Martínez Zaldo was a stockholder of the Banco Financiero and that José Guash Prieto and Amadeo Barletta Barletta were in possession of a stock portfolio.[9]

In relation to the barrage of insults and disrespectful statements that Lobo directed against Rendueles, it is interesting to observe how Dr. Eladio Ramírez León (Lobo's right-hand man) came out publicly as the most faithful friend of Rendueles.

As soon as Barletta's group began its operations in the Banco Financiero — the bank's board of directors later proposed that Barletta form part of the bank's leadership; but Barletta declined, preferring to remain in the shadows — the great business deals began for Lobo. On November 18, 1954, Special Decree 1800 was made public. This law, signed by General Batista, opened the fabulous financial scheme of the Ferrocarriles Occidentales de Cuba [Western Railroads of Cuba]. Only five days later, on November 23, 1954, Lobo was already convening a meeting of directors to inform them that their bank assumed the financing of stocks in the Ferrocarriles Occidentales de Cuba and that:

> …a number of companies that own and operate sugar mills have gone to the Banco Financiero to request loans to acquire and pay for opportune stocks declared eligible by the BNC. This loan has, in addition, by virtue of the decree that has been cited, the extra fee of three centavos per 325-pound sack or its equivalent created to that effect by the law.[10]
>
> These loans will be discounted in the BNC for the full value of the loans themselves at two percent interest annually. The private banks, for their part, will not be able to charge interest over four percent annually. These loans have and enjoy all exemptions from taxes and other facilities that the law has granted for financing sugar of the stabilizing quota. Regarding all of this, the president [Lobo] deems that private banks have a duty to cooperate with the government in solving a problem of great national interest. Furthermore, he feels that the loans are attractive in themselves as an investment by the bank because of the guarantees that they have and the facilities that the BNC offers for their rediscounting. Because of all this, he recommends to the board of directors that they approve the authorization of such loans to the degree that the resources of the Banco Financiero allow it.[11]

The credits were granted to a group of holding companies or companies affiliated with the Banco Financiero, or to companies that were in Lobo's realm of dominion. Besides offering a way of initiating control over the interests of the Ferrocarriles Occidentales de Cuba, this operation guaranteed that important sugar-producing areas and industries in the western provinces came under Lobo's influence. Until then, most of the sugar mills under his dominion were found in the province of Oriente.

The most astonishing thing, however, is that Lobo already had the business organized when this decree was made public. Five days later, he presented the list of credits that would be granted to the following sugar mills: Central San Cristóbal; Central Tinguaro; Central La Francia; Central Araujo; Central Perseverancia; Central Niquero; Central Cape Cruz; Compañía Tánamo de Cuba (Central Tánamo); Escambray Sugar Company (Central Escambray); Central Estrada Palma; Compañía Azucarera Jocuma (Central Covadonga); La Rancho Veloz Sugar Company; Central Hormiguero; Central Parque Alto and North American Sugar Company (Central Narcisa).

Immediately, José Manuel Martínez Zaldo received extremely generous treatment. Lobo assigned to him more than 2,000 pesos, monthly, in salary and commissions. Meanwhile, for the Christmas bonus that year the usually stingy Lobo set aside only 120 pesos for eight or nine prominent bank employees.[12]

In the proceedings of January 25, 1955, Lobo declared that his intention was to attract to the Banco Financiero "elements that were not precisely those interested in the sugar industry, but in other mercantile and commercial activities."[13]

On March 30, 1955, the Banco Financiero reported that it had received US$3 million more in deposits than it had in the previous period. It also reported that in its phase of expansion it would be opening or planned to open branches in Colón, Santo Domingo, Placetas, Nicaro, Tánamo, Rodas, Artemisa, Manzanillo, Marianao and other places in Havana.

Martínez Zaldo, for his part, reported that arrangements were being made so that the Banco Financiero might acquire, along with its "other friends," the Banco Carvajal in Artemisa. The negotiations for acquiring this bank were already quite advanced.[14] There was also talk of buying the branch (the building) of the City Bank of Manzanillo, and strong interest had been shown in FHA investments.[15]

At a meeting of the board of stockholders on March 30, 1955, Dr. Eladio Ramírez León mentioned an article by Cepero Bonilla that appeared in the newspaper *Prensa Libre*:

> [The article alleged that Lobo, by means of his bank] …had financed sugar mills that were not clients of the bank itself, so that the mills might pay for the stocks that belonged to him in the Ferrocarriles Occidentales de Cuba, on the condition that they give him the vote corresponding to those stocks to use in the designation of one of the representatives of the *hacendados* on the Board of Directors of said railroad, and for this reason the BNC had refused to approve said financing.[16]

Ramírez León affirmed that everything stated in the article was false. The BNC had approved the finances in each case; in each and every case that had been submitted. Lobo had not intervened in any way to gain this approval. "Several comments were made about this matter, but the general opinion prevailed that they would pretend not to know the news officially, and that they would be even less inclined to contradict it."[17]

By February 1956, Martínez Zaldo appeared as the official representative of the stock portfolio held by Amadeo Barletta Barletta and José Guash Prieto. In Record No. 28 of the proceedings of the Banco Financiero,[18] Lobo imposes a distribution of earnings that is surprising: 25 percent of the profits obtained by the bank as a consequence of its operations would pass directly to the president and the vice-president and to other executives they nominated.

The only stockholder who opposed this measure, albeit timidly, was Dr. Francisco Escobar Quezada who, quite logically, said he did not have "knowledge that such a thing was done as common practice in business affairs."[19] It was Lorido Lombardero himself (also now a stockholder in the Barletta-affiliated Banco Financiero) who came out in defense of Lobo's proposal, assuring that in the "insurance corporation of which he formed a part, 28 percent has been allocated for this purpose, to compensate the directors who work."[20]

In January 1956, deposits in the Banco Financiero reached more than US$5 million. By that date, and for the first time, the bank's records also affirmed that it would embark upon a grand-scale financial operation in Barletta's business affairs.[21]

At the same stockholders' meeting, Lobo assured that: "the situation of the country continues to be relatively comfortable, given that the sugar crop this year is superior to last year's, and the prices are maintained at attractive levels, not so much as to result in great profits, but enough to maintain business on an acceptable basis."[22]

By May 1956, the Banco Financiero had more than US$7 million in deposits and held a substantial quantity of veterans, tribunals and public works bonds; securities of the so-called Compañía Cubana de Electricidad (put into circulation by BANDES and other institutions). In addition, it maintained in assets more than US$1 million for new investments of this type.

In keeping with the report of the Cámara de Compensaciones del BNC, the Banco Financiero in April 1956 occupied ninth place among the 72 banks in the system (including the affiliates of the great U.S. banks in Cuba) with a total of US$17.5 million in effects presented and US$18.7 million in effects received, a reflection of the importance that "our bank continues to achieve daily."[23]

Without a doubt, 1956 was a completely satisfactory year for Lobo. If we consider operations in U.S. currency that went unreported, earnings have to be considerably greater. One must also consider that Lobo was about to receive important deposits from the Cuban Congress, from Cajas de Jubilaciones, from the Seguro del Retiro Azucarero and funds allocated for the construction of peasant dwellings, which would considerably increase the bank's financial potential.

Consequently, because of all these facts and its new position, it was logical that the Banco Financiero joined the U.S. Mafia's projects for the great hotel renovation of the empire of Havana.

Investments in the tourist center of Barlovento, known later as Monte Carlo de La Habana, were the first to be reported. This initial investment did not amount to a great sum for the Banco Financiero, because, in reality, the Cuban state almost entirely assumed the costs.

For a more precise idea of escalating Mafia business deals and ties with Cuban state institutions (such as BANDES, Banco de Comercio Exterior de Cuba, Financiero Nacional and other institutions) and with the Banco Financiero under Lobo and the Barletta family, Lobo's report to the general board of the bank stockholders, of April 23, 1957, explains:

> Immediately following, the president observed the state of affairs in the negotiations regarding the financing of the Hotel Habana Riviera [a hotel that is known internationally to be an operation of Meyer Lansky in Havana];[24] he expounded upon the project extensively and manifested that it was necessary to adopt an agreement designating functionaries of the Banco [Financiero] to accept in the bank's name the designation as fiduciary agents or trustees of the Comisión

de Bonos Valores Públicos Nacionales, which the Banco de Desarrollo Económico y Social will make.[25]

Connections with Lobo's bank also extended to numerous Mafia front companies; such as the company Hotelera de La Habana and the Compañía de Hoteles La Riviera de Cuba. Toward the end of the 1950s, these and other companies were rapidly expanding. They had begun construction of hotel complexes in the Cuban capital, Varadero, Cienfuegos, Isla de Pinos and the mountains of Pinar del Río, for the enjoyment of moneyed tourists accustomed to a fast pace. And by 1957-58, they were preparing for a second and greater expansion, which would include the construction of 50 great resort hotels, with sites from the banks of the Jaimanitas River to the beach at Varadero. The grand Hotel Monte Carlo de La Habana (currently the Marina Hemingway) was the beginning of this fabulous project. It is necessary to underscore, however, that the Barletta family (by the end of 1957 and surely as a part of this new expansion), initiated an apparent retreat from Lobo's bank, after first consolidating its interests and ties with the Banco Financiero. The Banco Financiero, however, still continued its operations with Mafia companies and businesses, even during 1959.

In the final days of 1957, José Manuel Martínez Zaldo presented his resignation as executive vice-president of the Banco Financiero. Without a doubt, it was a formal retirement. José Guash Prieto and Amadeo Barletta also retired. Their stock portfolios, and some portfolios held by others, were transferred to Lobo or to other front companies, all on the same date.

José Manuel Martínez Zaldo claimed he was retiring from the Banco Financiero due to serious health problems.[26] The bank's operations were, in an executive sense, at that moment totally in Zaldo's hands. Imagine the surprise when, just a few weeks later, it became known that Zaldo had been designated vice-president of the Banco Pedroso. This would extend the influence of the Mafia groups ruling the empire of Havana, and multiply their connections with the banking institutions that made up the international financial center in Havana.

Notes

Introduction

1. Frederic Sondern Jr., *Brotherhood of Evil: The Mafia* (New York: Farrar, Straus and Cudahy, 1959), p. 167.

Chapter I

1. *Bohemia* magazine, "En Cuba" section, Havana, September 8, 1957, pp. 76-77.
2. R. Hunt Phillips, *New York Times*, 1957.
3. Juan Almeida Bosque wrote three books entitled *Presidio, Exilio,* and *Desembarco*: they were published in Havana by Editorial Ciencias Sociales in 1986, 1987 and 1988, respectively.
4. *Bohemia* magazine, Havana, June 14, 1957, p. 74.
5. *Bohemia* magazine, Havana, August 4, 1957.
6. Archivo Nacional de Cuba, records of the BNC, Files 591 and 526, Numbers 16 and 17, respectively.
7. Sondern Jr., p. 15.

Chapter II

1. Archivo Nacional de Cuba, records of the BNC, File 160, Number 30.
2. Gregorio Ortega, *La coletilla* (Havana: Editora Política, 1989), pp. 168-169.
3. Enrique Cirules, "La mafia norteamericana en Cuba: operaciones y fraudes," *Bohemia* magazine, Havana, October 11, 1991, pp. 15-17.
4. Martin A. Gosch and Richard Hammer, *The Last Testament of Lucky Luciano* (Boston: Little, Brown and Company, 1974), p. 169.
5. Enrique Cirules, "Trafficante: la era de la cocaína," *Bohemia* magazine, Havana, October 25, 1991, pp. 14-15.
6. Gosch and Hammer, pp. 169-171.
7. Hortensia Pichardo, *Documentos para la historia de Cuba* (Havana: Editorial Ciencias Sociales, 1971), p. 513.

8. Julio Le Riverend, *La república, dependencia y revolución* (Havana: Instituto del Libro, 1966), p. 229.
9. Author's note.
10. Fulgencio Batista, *Paradojismo* (Mexico City: Ediciones Botas, 1964), pp. 40-42.
11. Oscar Pino-Santos, *Cuba, historia y economía* (Havana: Editorial Ciencias Sociales, 1983), p. 470.
12. Mario J. Arango and Jorge V. Child, *Narcotráfico, imperio de la cocaína* (Mexico City: Editorial Diana, 1984), p. 116.
13. Author's note.
14. Benigno Iglesias Trabadelo, *El primero de enero y el Hotel Deauville* (unpublished manuscript), author's archive, p. 11.
15. Archivo Nacional de Cuba, records of the BNC, File 192, Number 6.
16. Penny Lernoux, *In Banks We Trust* (Garden City, New York: Anchor Press/Doubleday, 1984), p. 81.
17. Lyman B. Kirkpatrick, *The Real CIA* (New York: Macmillan, 1968), p. 156.
18. Arango and Child, p. 116.
19. Archivo Nacional de Cuba, records of the BNC, File 192, Number 7.
20. *Ibid.*
21. Portfolio from the Banco Gelats containing correspondence with U.S. banks, author's archive.
22. Archivo Nacional de Cuba, records of the BNC, Book 232, Number 1, Documents 18-43.
23. Eduardo R. Chibás, *Luz* newspaper, Havana, 1937.
24. U.S. Congress on Latin America, "Nixon and Organized Crime," *NACLA's Latin American and Empire Report,* Special Issue — Nixon and the Election, Volume 6, Number 8, page 5, New York, October 1972.
25. *Bohemia* magazine, "En Cuba" section, Havana, April 3, 1944.
26. *Bohemia* magazine, Havana, June 11, 1944, p. 21.
27. *Bohemia* magazine, Havana, September 10, 1944.

Chapter III

1. Enrique Cirules, "Los negocios de don Amleto," *Bohemia* magazine, Havana, October 18, 1991, pp. 13-17.
2. Antonio Gil Carballo, "El tráfico de drogas en Cuba," *Bohemia* magazine, Havana, October 8, 1944, pp. 70-71.
3. Gosch and Hammer, p. 305.
4. *Bohemia* magazine, "En Cuba" section, Havana, December 8, 1946, p. 45.

5. Gosch and Hammer, p. 312.
6. Anthony Summers, *Goddess: The Secret Lives of Marilyn Monroe* (New York: Macmillan, 1985), p. 106.
7. Gosch and Hammer, pp. 322-323.
8. Gosch and Hammer, p. 323.
9. Sondern Jr., p. 115.
10. *Ibid.*
11. *Ibid.*
12. *Ibid.*
13. Sondern Jr., pp. 115-116.
14. Sondern Jr., p. 116.
15. Sondern Jr., p. 115.
16. Harry J. Anslinger, "Foreword," *The Brotherhood of Evil: The Mafia,* by Frederic Sondern Jr. (New York: Farrar, Straus and Cudahy, 1959), page ix.
17. Author's note.
18. Sondern Jr., pp. 115-116.
19. Author's note.
20. Sondern Jr., p. 116.
21. *Ibid.*
22. Gosch and Hammer, pp. 324-325.
23. Sondern Jr., p. 116.

Chapter IV
1. *Bohemia* magazine, "En Cuba" section, Havana, January 14, 1945.
2. *Bohemia* magazine, "En Cuba" section, Havana, May 2, 1948, p. 56.
3. Guillermo Alonso Pujol, "Ante la historia," *La corrupción política y administrativa en Cuba,* E. Vignier and G. Alonso, editors (Havana: Editorial Ciencias Sociales, 1973), pp. 300-301.
4. *Ibid.*
5. *Bohemia* magazine, "En Cuba" section, Havana, May 20, 1948, p. 81.

Chapter V
1. Fidel Castro, "Informe de Fidel Castro al Tribunal de Cuentas," *Alerta* newspaper, Havana, March 4, 1952, pp. 1 and 7.
2. Pelayo Cuervo Navarro, "Historiando fraudes," *Bohemia* magazine, Havana, November 7, 1948.
3. *Ibid.*
4. E. Vignier and G. Alonso, editors, *La corrupción política y administrativa en Cuba* (Havana: Editorial Ciencias Sociales, 1973).

5. Pino-Santos, pp. 542-549.
6. U.S. Senate Commission directed by the Democratic Senator from the Tennessee, Estes Kefauver, who investigated organized crime in the United States between 1950-51.
7. Sondern Jr., p. 167.
8. Estes Kefauver, *Crime in America* (Garden City, New York: Doubleday, 1951), p. 12-16. (Frederic Sondern Jr. says, on page 168 of *Brotherhood of Evil: The Mafia*, referring to Kefauver's book, "For some reason it never received the attention it deserved.")
9. Sondern Jr., p. 170.
10. Sondern Jr., p. 174.
11. Sondern Jr., p. 187.
12. Orestes Ferrara, "Carta a Guillermo Alonso Pujol," *Bohemia* magazine, Havana, January 14, 1951, p. 63.
13. Gosch and Hammer, 1974, p. 349.
14. In the article "Ante la Historia," by Guillermo Alonso Pujol, written after the coup d'état of 1952, and published in Havana in *Bohemia* magazine on 5 October 1952, on pp. 60-63 and 90, the author tries to manipulate the facts concerning these events. Furthermore, he makes it apparent that Vice-President Prío's relationship with Batista was extremely confidential, and protected by a long-standing and deep friendship.
15. *Bohemia* magazine, "En Cuba" section, Havana, July 22, 1951, p. 72.
16. *Bohemia* magazine, "En Cuba" section, Havana, August 5, 1951, p. 75.
17. *Bohemia* magazine, "En Cuba" section, Havana, July 29, 1951, p. 67.
18. *Ibid.*
19. "La violenta polémica Chibás-Sánchez Arango," *Bohemia* magazine, Havana, July 29, 1951, p. 76.
20. "Tiene que cumplir su destino histórico," *Bohemia* magazine, Havana, August 12, 1951.
21. Alonso Pujol, *loc. cit.*, p. 60.

Chapter VI

1. *Informe Central al Primer Congreso del Partido Comunista de Cuba*, Havana, Edición DOR, 1975, p. 21.
2. David Wise and Thomas B. Ross, *The Invisible Government* (New York: Random House, 1964), p. 93.
3. Lernoux, p. 77.
4. Sondern Jr., pp. 111-112.
5. Wise and Ross, p. 94.
6. Wise and Ross, p. 4. (Speech by Allen Dulles at Yale University on February 3, 1958).

7. Wise and Ross, p. 100.
8. Pino-Santos, p. 548.
9. Wise and Ross, p. 7.
10. Le Riverend, p. 354.
11. Alonso Pujol, *op. cit.* pp. 302-303.
12. E. Vignier and G. Alonso, editors, *op. cit.*, Report to the chief of the Department of Administration of the SIM. (Servicio de Inteligencia Militar, or Military Intelligence Service), dated February 8, 1952, signed by Captain Salvador Díaz-Verson Rodríguez, who was connected also to the CIA and the FBI.
13. *Bohemia* magazine, "En Cuba" section, Havana, 5 August 1951, pp. 75-77.
14. Blas Roca, *Fundamentos*, Havana, May 1952, Year XII, Number 122, p. 393.
15. *Ibid.*
16. *Ibid.*

Chapter VII

1. Archivo Nacional de Cuba, records of the BNC, File 192, Number 6.
2. *Ibid.*
3. *Ibid.*
4. *Ibid.*
5. *Ibid.*
6. *Ibid.*
7. *Ibid.*
8. Archivo Nacional de Cuba, records of the BNC, File 192, Number 7.
9. *Ibid.*
10. *Ibid.*
11. *Ibid.*
12. *Ibid.*
13. *Ibid.*
14. *Ibid.*
15. *Ibid.*
16. *Ibid.*
17. Cirules, "La mafia norteamericana en Cuba (...), *op. cit.*, pp. 15-17.
18. Other limited liability companies with which the Barletta group conducted substantial operations were: Sucesores de Rivero y Méndez, Troncoso y Ferrón, Automotriz Ania, California Luncheonettes, Inc., Camayd Autos, Compañía Constructora Llama, Compañía Proveedora de Helados, Concreto Caribe, Demestre y Compañía, Inversiones,

Inversiones G. Casal Atlántida, Madonna Hermanos, Malaret Insurance Office, Mion Luis, Víctor G. Vries, and the Compañía de Contratos y Negociaciones.

19. Other insitutions with which the Banco Atlántico engaged in important business affairs were: Palacio de la TV, La Cueva, El Relámpago, Autos y Camiones, Proveedora Dental, Plastic Crom Import Company, Tipografía J. Suárez, Unión Radio Televisión, Autos Riviera, Bennony Trading Company, Unión Radio, and Televisora Panorama, under the charge of Giovanni Spada.

20. Sondern Jr., pp. 14-15.

21. Sondern Jr., p. 15.

Chapter VIII

1. Le Riverend, p. 340.

2. *Ibid.*

3. *Ibid.*

4. Le Riverend, p. 343.

5. *Ibid.*

6. Le Riverend, p. 344.

7. Le Riverend, p. 346.

8. Le Riverend, p. 348.

9. María Caridad Pacheco González, "Situación de los obreros industriales cubanos en víspera de la revolución," *Revista Cubana de Ciencias Sociales,* Havana, 1990, p. 100.

10. Francis Adams Truslow, *et al., Report on Cuba* (Baltimore: The Johns Hopkins Press, 1951), p. 13.

11. Truslow, *et al.,* pp. 15 and 20.

12. *Bohemia* magazine, Havana, December 9, 1991, p. 61.

13. BANDES was created by Decree Number 1589 on August 4, 1954.

14. Letter from the Director of the CIA, Allen Dulles, to General Fulgencio Batista, July 15, 1955, Archivo Museo del Ministerio del Interior.

15. Decree Number 1589, *Gaceta Oficial de Cuba,* Havana, January 27, 1955. Taken from Erasmo Dumpierre's *El BANDES: corrupción y política,* Serie Histórica, No. 20 (Havana: Academia de Ciencias de Cuba, Instituto de Historia, 1970), pp. 3-4.

16. *Ibid.*

17. Fulgencio Batista, *Paradoja* (Mexico City: Ediciones Botas, 1963), pp. 213, 217-219.

18. Other companies were: Goodyear Rubber & Tire Company; General Electric Company; Owen Illinois Glass Company; Phelps Dodger

Company (copper); International Telegraph and Telephone Company; Standard Electric of Cuba; Republic Steel Company; Reynolds Metal Corporation; Texaco Company; and Standard Oil of New Jersey, which belonged to the powerful Rockefeller consortium.

19. Erasmo Dumpierre, *El BANDES: corrupción y política*, Serie Histórica, No. 20 (Havana: Academia de Ciencias de Cuba, Instituto de Historia, 1970), p. 25.
20. Dumpierre, pp. 18-20.

Chapter IX
1. "Havana," film directed by Sydney Pollack, Universal, 1990.

Chapter X
1. Archivo Nacional de Cuba, records of the BNC, File 526, Number 7.
2. Author's archive, Libro del Gabinete de Identificación (Register of the Bureau of Identification) for the registration of Foreigners' Identification Cards.
3. Author's archive, testimony of witness who has requested anonymity.
4. Sondern Jr., p. 15.
5. Iglesias Trabadelo, in author's archive.
6. Author's archive, payrolls of the Casino of the Hotel Habana Hilton that indicate payments to Social Security of Cuba.
7. Testimony of one of the instructors at one of the dealers' schools in Havana, author's archive.
8. Archivo Nacional de Cuba, records of the BNC, File 526, Number 7, addenda.
9. Author's note.
10. Sondern Jr., p. 7.
11. Author's archive, testimonies about Meyer Lansky in Havana. For personal reasons, the witness has preferred anonymity.
12. Sondern Jr., p. 7.
13. Author's note.
14. Author's note.
15. Sondern Jr., pp. 14-15.

Chapter XI
1. Archivo Nacional de Cuba, records of the BNC, File 591, Number 16.
2. *Ibid.*
3. Archivo Nacional de Cuba, records of the BNC, File 526, Number 7.
4. Archivo Nacional de Cuba, records of the BNC, File 591, Number 16.

5. Archivo Nacional de Cuba, records of the BNC, File 526, Number 7 (Report to BANDES from a group of lawyers tied to the Mafia).
6. *Ibid.*
7. *Ibid.*
8. *Ibid.*
9. *Ibid.*
10. *Ibid.*
11. *Ibid.*
12. Author's emphasis.
13. Archivo Nacional de Cuba, records of the BNC, File 526, Number 7 (Report to BANDES from a group of lawyers tied to the Mafia).
14. Author's note.
15. Author's note.
16. Archivo Nacional de Cuba, records of the BNC, File 526, Number 7.
17. *Ibid.*

Chapter XII

1. Dwight D. Eisenhower, *The White House Years: Waging Peace (1956-1961)* (Garden City, New York: Doubleday, 1965), p. 520.
2. F. Sergueev, *La guerra secreta contra Cuba* (Moscow: Editorial Progreso, 1982), pp. 28-29.
3. Eisenhower, p. 521.
4. Author's note.
5. Lernoux, p. 107.
6. Lernoux, p. 77.
7. "Autobuses," *Bohemia* magazine, "En Cuba" section, Havana, 30 September 1951, p. 73.
8. U.S. Senate, *Communist Threat to the United States Through the Caribbean* (Washington: U.S. Government Printing Office, 1960), p. 739. Taken from the Testimony of William D. Pawley during the Hearings before the Subcommittee To Investigate the Administration of the Internal Security Act and Other Internal Security Laws, Committee on the Judiciary, U.S. Senate, 86th Congress, 2nd session, Part 10, September 2, 1960.
9. Wise and Ross, p. 99.
10. Sergueev, p. 28.
11. Earl E. T. Smith, *The Fourth Floor* (1962; Washington: Selous Foundation Press, 1990), p. 170.
12. Smith, pp. 172 and 176.
13. Roberto Orihuela, *Nunca fui un traidor* (Havana: Editorial Capitán San Luis, 1991), pp. 131-132, 152-153.
14. *Frente Camagüey* (Havana: Editora Política, 1958).

Appendix One

1. Archivo Nacional de Cuba, records of the BNC, File 493, Number 5.
2. *Ibid.*
3. *Ibid.*
4. *Ibid.*
5. *Ibid.*
6. *Ibid.*
7. Author's note.
8. Archivo Nacional de Cuba, records of the BNC, File 493, Number 5.
9. Author's note.
10. Archivo Nacional de Cuba, records of the BNC, File 493, Number 5.
11. Archivo Nacional de Cuba, records of the BNC, File 520, Number 15.
12. *Ibid.*
13. *Ibid.*
14. Author's archive, payrolls from the Casino of the Hilton Hotel Internacional (Havana Hilton) reflecting payments to Social Security of Cuba, July 1958.
15. Iglesias Trabadelo in author's archive.
16. Iglesias Trabadelo, p. 44.
17. Iglesias Trabadelo, p. 20.
18. *Ibid.*
19. Iglesias Trabadelo, p. 30.
20. Iglesias Trabadelo, p. 37.
21. Sondern Jr., pp. 14-15.
22. Author's note.
23. Archivo Nacional de Cuba, records of the BNC, File 517, Number 17.
24. *Ibid.*
25. *Ibid.*
26. *Ibid.*
27. Author's note.
28. Author's note.
29. Author's emphasis.
30. Author's archive, letter from Dr. Eladio Ramírez León, vice-president of the Banco Financiero, to Dr. Felipe Pazos, president of the BNC, July 6, 1959.

Appendix Two

1. Archivo Nacional de Cuba, records of the BNC, File 202, No. 12.
2. *Ibid.*
3. Directorio Telefónico de Cuba, Havana, July 1937, advertisement leaf between pp. 74 and 75.

4. Archivo Nacional de Cuba, records of the BNC, Book 232, p. 31. The message is dated June 19, 1953.
5. Archivo Nacional de Cuba, records of the BNC, Book 232, Document 10, February 17, 1954.
6. *Ibid.*
7. Archivo Nacional de Cuba, records of the BNC, Book 232, Volume I, p. 41.
8. Archivo Nacional de Cuba, records of the BNC, Book 232, Meeting of June 17, 1954.
9. *Ibid.*
10. Archivo Nacional de Cuba, records of the BNC, Book 232, Document 16.
11. *Ibid.*
12. Archivo Nacional de Cuba, records of the BNC, Book 232, Document 17, December 15, 1954.
13. Archivo Nacional de Cuba, records of the BNC, Book 232, Record of January 25, 1955.
14. Archivo Nacional de Cuba, records of the BNC, Book 232, Document 20, March 10, 1955 (Extraordinary Meeting of Council of Directors).
15. *Ibid.*
16. *Ibid.*
17. *Ibid.*
18. Archivo Nacional de Cuba, records of the BNC, Book 232, Document 28, February 8, 1956.
19. *Ibid.*
20. *Ibid.*
21. Archivo Nacional de Cuba, records of the BNC, Book 232, Document 27 (Extraordinary Meeting of Council of Directors).
22. *Ibid.*
23. Archivo Nacional de Cuba, records of the BNC, Book 232, Volume I, Document 29 (Meeting of Council of Directors, May 9, 1956).
24. Sondern Jr., p. 14.
25. Archivo Nacional de Cuba, records of the BNC, Book 232, Volume I, Document 38, April 23, 1957, p. 165.
26. Archivo Nacional de Cuba, records of the BNC, Book 232, Volume I, Document 42, pp. 174-175 (José Martínez Zaldo resigned as executive vice-president of Banco Financiero on December 17, 1957).

Bibliography

ALMEIDA BOSQUE, JUAN. *Presidio*. Havana: Editorial Ciencias Sociales, 1986.

—. *Exilio*. Havana: Editorial Ciencias Sociales, 1987.

—. *Desembarco*. Havana: Editorial Ciencias Sociales, 1988.

ARANGO, MARIO J., AND CHILD V. JORGE. *Narcotráfico, imperio de la cocaína*. Mexico City: Editorial Diana, 1984.

BÁEZ, LUIS. *Los que se fueron*. Havana: Editorial José Martí, 1991.

BATISTA, FULGENCIO. *Respuesta*. Mexico City: Ediciones Botas, 1960.

—. *Paradoja*. Mexico City: Ediciones Botas, 1963.

—. *Paradojismo*. Mexico City: Ediciones Botas, 1964.

BONSAL, PHILIP W. *Cuba, Castro, and the United States*. Pittsburgh: University of Pittsburgh Press, 1971.

CASTRO RUZ, FIDEL. *La historia me absolverá*. Havana: Editora Política, 1963.

CASTILLO, FABIO. *Los jinetes de la cocaína*. Bogotá: Editorial Documentos Periodísticos, 1987.

COLLAZC PÉREZ, ENRIQUE. *Banca y crédito*. Havana: Editorial Ciencias Sociales, 1989

DUMPIERRE, ERASMO. *El BANDES: corrupción y política*. Serie Histórica, No. 20. Havana: Academia de Ciencias de Cuba, Instituto de Historia, 1970.

EISENHOWER, DWIGHT D. *The White House Years: Waging Peace (1956-1961)*. Garden City, New York: Doubleday, 1965.

ESPINOZA GARCÍA, MANUEL. *La política económica de los Estados Unidos hacia América Latina entre 1945 y 1961*. Havana: Premio Ensayo Casa de las Americas, 1971.

FERRERA HERRERA, ALBERTO. *El Granma: la aventura del siglo*. Havana: Editorial Capitán San Luis, 1991.

GÁLVEZ, WILLIAM. *Camilo: señor de la vanguardia*. Havana: Editorial Ciencias Sociales, 1979.

GOSCH, MARTIN A., AND RICHARD HAMMER. *The Last Testament of Lucky Luciano*. Boston: Little, Brown and Company, 1974.

HORVATH, RICARDO. *Cuba, la oculta*. Havana: Editorial Pablo de la Torriente, 1987.

IGLESIAS TRABADELO, BENIGNO. *El primero de enero y el Hotel Deauville.* Unpublished manuscript. Author's archive.

JULIEN, CLAUDE. *El Imperio norteamericano.* Havana: Editorial Ciencias Sociales, 1970.

KEFAUVER, ESTES. *Crime in America.* Garden City, New York: Doubleday, 1951.

KIRKPATRICK, LYMAN B. *The Real CIA.* New York: Macmillan, 1968.

KOLEV, JRISTO. *La "cosa nostra."* Havana: Editorial Ciencias Sociales, 1989.

KUCHILÁN, MARIO. *Fabulario, retrato de una época.* Havana: Instituto del Libro, 1970.

LEÓN TORRAS, RAÚL. *Antología.* Havana: Editorial de Ciencias Sociales, 1988.

LE RIVEREND, JULIO. *La república, dependencia y revolución.* Havana: Instituto del Libro, 1966.

LERNOUX, PENNY. *In Banks We Trust.* Garden City, New York: Anchor Press/ Doubleday, 1984.

LENIN, V. I. *El estado y la revolución.* Havana: Imprenta Nacional de Cuba.

ORIHUELA, ROBERTO. *Nunca fui un traidor.* Havana: Editorial Capitán San Luis, 1991.

ORTEGA, GREGORIO. *La coletilla.* Havana: Editora Política, 1989.

ORTEGÓN PÁEZ, RAFAEL. *Vorágine alucinante de las drogas.* Bogotá : Ediciones Tercer Mundo, 1981.

PACHECO GONZÁLEZ, MARÍA CARIDAD. "Situación de los obreros industriales en víspera de la Revolución." (Historical research.) *Revista Cubana de Ciencias Sociales* [Havana] Year XXIV. No. VIII. pp. 100-117.

PICHARDO, HORTENSIA. *Documentos para la historia de Cuba.* Havana: Editorial Ciencias Sociales, 1971.

PINO-SANTOS, OSCAR. *Cuba, historia y economía.* Havana: Editorial Ciencias Sociales, 1983.

PUZO, MARIO. *The Godfather.* New York: G.P. Putnam's Sons, 1969.

PORTILLA, JUAN. *Jesús Menéndez y su tiempo.* Havana: Editorial Ciencias Sociales, 1987.

SARRACINO, RODOLFO. *El grupo Rockefeller actúa.* Havana: Editorial Ciencias Sociales, 1987.

SERGUEEV, F. *La guerra secreta contra Cuba.* Moscow: Editorial Progreso, 1982.

SMITH, EARL E. T. *The Fourth Floor.* 1962. Washington: Selous Foundation Press, 1990.

SONDERN, FREDERIC JR. *Brotherhood of Evil: The Mafia.* New York: Farrar, Straus and Cudahy, 1959.

SUMMERS, ANTHONY. *Goddess: The Secret Lives of Marilyn Monroe.* New York: Macmillan, 1985.

TABARES DEL REAL, JOSÉ A. *La Revolución del 30: sus dos últimos años.* Havana: Editorial Ciencias Sociales, 1973.

TRUSLOW, FRANCIS ADAMS, *ET AL. Report on Cuba.* Baltimore: The Johns Hopkins Press, 1951.

TURKUS, BURTON B., AND SID FEDER. *Murder, Inc.: The Story of "the Syndicate."* New York: Farrar, Straus and Young, 1951.

VARGAS CHACÓN, FELIX. *40 años en el delito.* Caracas: "Memorias del Cumanés," 1974.

VIGNIER, E., AND G. ALONSO, EDITORS. *La corrupción política y administrativa en Cuba.* Havana: Editorial Ciencias Sociales, 1973.

WISE, DAVID, AND THOMAS B. ROSS. *The Invisible Government.* New York: Random House, 1964.

Other Sources Consulted

Records of the BNC in the Archivo Nacional de Cuba.

Payrolls of the defunct Archivo de Seguridad Social de Cuba, of the casinos, Hipódromo, clubs and cabarets of the U.S. Mafia. (Author's archive).

Periodical press of the era (1934-58).

Telephone directories (1934-58).

Bohemia magazine. Especially the study of the "En Cuba" section during the 1940s and 1950s.

Informe Central al Primer Congreso del Partido Comunista de Cuba. Havana, 1975.

Frente Camagüey. Havana: Editora Política, 1958.

Directorio Bancario de Cuba. Published by the Asociación de Bancos de Cuba. Havana, 1954-55.

De Eisenhower a Reagan. (Series of analyses by various Cuban authors about political policies of the United States against Cuba). Havana: Editorial Ciencias Sociales, 1987.

U.S. Congress on Latin America. "Nixon and Organized Crime." *NACLA's Latin America & Empire Report, Special Issue − Nixon and the Election. Volume VI, Number 8, p. 3-17. New York, October 1972.*

Commercial Directory of the municipality of Havana, 1958.

Havana Chronicle magazine. Published by the Comisión Nacional de Turismo. Havana: 1941-42.

Moncada, antecedentes y preparativos. Vol. I. Havana: Editora Política, 1985.

"Havana." Film directed by Sydney Pollack. Universal, 1990.

AFROCUBA

An Anthology of Cuban Writing on Race, Politics and Culture

*Edited by Jean Stubbs
and Pedro Pérez Sarduy*

An insightful look at Cuba's rich ethnic and cultural reality

What is it like to be black in Cuba? Does racism exist in a revolutionary society that claims to have abolished it? How does the legacy of slavery and segregation live on in today's Cuba?

Essays, poetry, extracts from novels, anthropological studies and political analysis are brought together by editors Jean Stubbs and Pedro Pérez to create an outstanding anthology of Cuban scholars, writers and artists. Drawing on an extensive knowledge of Cuba, the editors have produced a multi-faceted insight into Cuba's rich ethnic and cultural reality.

The book is divided into three sections: "The Die is Cast," "Myth and Reality" and "Redrawing the Line," introducing the reader to a wide range of previously unavailable Cuban authors, in which dissenting voices speak alongside established writers, such as Fernando Ortiz.

"For the non-Spanish speaking reader with an interest in either Caribbean history, or more specifically that of Cuba, Pedro Pérez Sarduy and Jean Stubbs have produced an indispensable anthology which may become a standard reference book." —**Caryl Phillips**

"The editors have brought together a rich portrait of AfroCuba, one of the most vibrant and—from an Anglo-Saxon point of view—least well-documented of the black Caribbean diasporas."—**Stuart Hall**

"One of the most complete anthologies to be published in English on race, politics and Cuban cultural roots." —*Granma International*

ISBN 978-1-875284-41-2 (paper)

CUBA: A HISTORY

Sergio Guerra Vilaboy and
Oscar Loyola Vega

A concise, readable history of Cuba beyond the images of salsa, cigars and classic cars

Beginning with the pre-Hispanic period, through to Cuba's struggle to maintain the revolution in the years following the collapse of the Soviet Union, and finally ending with Fidel Castro's decision to step down in 2008, this slim volume provides the reader with an overview of the history and politics of the tiny Caribbean island that so often has been at the center of world events.

Cuba: A History is an essential introduction to Cuba for students, visitors and others, explaining why the island has infuriated and enthralled its northern neighbors for centuries.

"The most beautiful island that eyes ever beheld." —**Christopher Columbus**

"Cuba has the same effect on U.S. administrations as the full moon has on wolves: it's an obsession." —**Wayne Smith**, former US diplomat in Havana

"I'm so grateful to see a place on the planet where there are people whose hearts haven't been shriveled by hatred or greed." —**Alice Walker**

ISBN 978-0-980429-24-4

Also available in Spanish ISBN 978-1-921438-60-8

CUBAN REVOLUTION READER

A Documentary History of Fidel Castro's Revolution

Edited by Julio García Luis

A timely new publication assessing 50 years of the Cuban revolution

The Cuban revolution was one of the defining moments of the 20th century, its influence reaching far beyond the shores of the tiny Caribbean island.

As Cuba marks the 50th anniversary of the 1959 overthrow of the Batista dictatorship, this book documents the turbulent history of Fidel Castro's revolution, from the euphoria of the early years to near economic collapse in the 1990s, and finally the Cuban leader's decision to step down in 2008.

The editor, Julio García Luis, offers a critical examination of Cuba's decades-long relationship with the Soviet Union and the epilogue considers the prospects for the revolution without Fidel Castro.

Including a comprehensive chronology and index, this is an essential resource for scholars and others.

"Cuba has lived a dramatic life with successes as well as failures. Alone and abandoned by all after the Soviet Union disappeared, it had to resist heroically some very hard years during which the United States intensified its economic and political aggression. Today Cuba forges a path to craft its own unique socialist system, rooted on its own historical experience and with the active participation of its people."
—**Ricardo Alarcón**

ISBN 978-1-920888-89-3 (paper)

Also available in Spanish ISBN 978-1-920888-08-4

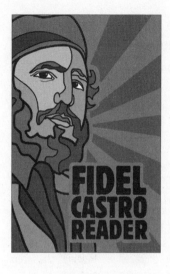

FIDEL CASTRO READER

Edited by David Deutschmann
and Deborah Shnookal

**An outstanding new anthology of one
of history's greatest orators**

At last! A comprehensive selection of one of the
20th century's most influential political figures and
one of history's greatest orators, Fidel Castro.

Opening with Fidel's famous courtroom defense
speech following the 1953 attack on the Moncada
garrison, this anthology includes more than five
decades of Fidel's outstanding oratory, right up to
his recent reflections on the future of the Cuban
revolution "post-Fidel."

With an extensive chronology on the Cuban revolution, a comprehensive index and
24 pages of photos, this is an essential resource for scholars, researchers and
general readers.

As new leaders and social forces emerge in Latin America today, this book sheds light
on the continent's future as well as its past.

ISBN 978-1-920888-88-6 (paper)

Also available in Spanish ISBN 978-1-921438-01-1

TRAVELERS TALES OF OLD CUBA
From Treasure Island to Mafia Den
Edited by John Jenkins

An evocative and entertaining selection of travel writing about pre-revolutionary Cuba

Few places are as fascinating as Cuba, which has drawn travelers ever since it was "discovered" by Columbus in 1492. Magnificently evoking the romance and drama as well as darker episodes of slavery and tyranny, this selection of journal entries, essays and guidebook commentaries begins in the days when Havana sheltered Caribbean pirate treasure ships and was the gateway to the Spanish empire in the New World.

Later chapters reflect the "American era" when the island was transformed into a glittering tourist and gambler's paradise operated by the Mafia.

Good travelers' stories should not only inform the reader but also fire the imagination. These tales are full of the flavor and manners of a bygone era, reflecting the various impressions of visitors to one of the most alluring islands on earth.

"Creating both a literary project and an historical mini-course on the early nineteenth to middle twentieth century, the editor has gathered writings mostly by Americans in Cuba who tended to have a complex 'love/hate relationship' with the place… In the end, most reveal their fondness for Cuba…" —*Foreword* magazine

ISBN 978-0-9804292-1-3